GOD'S WORD

A Personal and Political Challenge

Michele + Donna
Best Wishes

Peter J Carli

First published by Dog Ear Publishing
4011 Vincennes Road
Indianapolis, IN 46268
www.dogearpublishing.net

ISBN: 978-1-4575-4831-4

This book is printed on acid free paper.
Printed in the United States of America

In Memoriam

My parents who provided a safe, secure home, and handed on their faith and values.

My brother Jim, who touched the lives of many as a dedicated educator.

Fr. Thomas Doyle, SS, my mentor and friend, who challenged me to use my God-given talents.

Acknowledgements

My loving wife Carol, for her support and critical analysis in helping to edit this manuscript.

My brother Don, for his encouragement and the time he dedicated in editing my grammar and sentence structure.

The many scripture scholars who have dedicated their lives to the study of the Bible. I especially wish to mention Walter Brueggemann, Marcus Borg, John Dominic Crossan and Dr. Kenneth Bailey.

CONTENTS

POWER OF THE WORD

God said: "Let there be light," and there was light(Gn. 1:3).[1]

The word of the Lord has brought me derision and reproach all day. I say to myself, I will not mention him; I will speak his name no more. But then it becomes like a fire burning in my heart, imprisoned in my bones; I grow weary holding it in; I cannot endure it (Jer. 20:8-9).

Though the grass withers and the flower wilts, the word of our God stands forever (Is. 40:8).

For just as from the heavens the rain and snow come down and do not return there until they have watered the earth, making it fertile and fruitful, giving seed to him who sows and bread to him who eats, so shall my word be that goes forth from my mouth; it shall not return to me void, but shall do my will, achieving the end for which I sent it (Is. 55:10-11).

Indeed, the word of God is living and effective, sharper than any two-edged sword, penetrating even between soul and spirit, joints and marrow, and able to discern reflections and thoughts of the heart (Heb. 4:12).

You cannot imprison the word of the Lord(2 Tm. 2:9).[2]

The Word became flesh and made his dwelling among us. (Jn. 1:14).

PROLOGUE

The Bible is an amazing collection of various forms of inspired literature gathered over a period of 1,100 years reflecting God's revelation and our slowly developing consciousness. The journey takes us from the Garden of Eden to the New Jerusalem, a paradise of harmony with all of God's creatures to a city with streets lined with gold and walls built of precious jewels. Those two idyllic settings are only bookends to the myriad of stories revealing the divine presence amidst the good, the bad and the ugly of daily living.

As a Christian I believe there are two Books of Divine Revelation. The composition of the first began 14.7 billion years ago with an explosion that initiated the Divine dance which continues to unfold today. The writing of the second book began approximately three thousand years ago and ended around 120 CE.

The Bible is more of a library than a single book reflecting various literary forms, historical accounts, political, economic, legal and theological viewpoints. The Hebrew Bible (Old Testament) purports to cover the beginning of creation to 100 years before Christ. The New Testament, the distinctively Christian part of the Bible, reflects the life of Jesus and the development of the Christian Church until about 120 CE.

The Bible has had a profound impact on human history. On the one hand the sacred writings have inspired religious and civil institutions to promote more just and equitable societies. It has inspired numerous men and women to great heroism in the face of evil. Dietrich Bonhoeffer and many others died for their opposition to the Nazis. Martin Luther King Jr. was assassinated for his non-violent opposition to civil injustice. Philip and Daniel Berrigan willingly accepted prison terms for their prophetic opposition to the Vietnam War and nuclear armaments. It has inspired artists such as Michelangelo, Da Vinci and Raphael, and musicians such as Handel, Mozart and Beethoven. On the other hand, it has been used to justify horrendous evils: war, genocide, slavery, the rape of the environment, anti-Semitism, the subjugation of women, discrimination based on creed, race, economic status and sexual orientation. A key question that only history can answer is: "Has the Bible been a source of greater good or evil?"

Catholics, Orthodox and Protestants differ over the number of inspired books in the Old Testament. The Protestant traditions follow the Jewish canon, which recognized 39 books written in Hebrew. Since most early Christians spoke Greek, the Catholic and Orthodox traditions follow the Greek version of the Old Testament known as the Septuagint, which contained 46 books. The additional books are Tobit, Judith, 1&2 Maccabees, Wisdom, Ecclesiasticus, Baruch and some additional Greek passages in Daniel and Esther. Orthodox Christians also accept 1 & 2 Esdras, the prayer of Manasseh, Psalm 151 and 3 Maccabees. All Christians agree on the 27 books of the New Testament.

Those scholars who study the Bible view the sacred writings from two differing schools of thought. Fundamentalists believe that God dictated every word of the Bible to a human author who acted as a stenographer. Therefore, they not only believe every word is inspired, but the texts are an infallible source of information. They believe that the Bible can only be interpreted literally.

Catholic and mainline Protestant scholars also believe that the Bible is inspired, but that God used human authors to reveal the Divine plan for humanity. Therefore, each book needs to be understood in its historical, sociological and political context to comprehend the revelation that God intended the human author to communicate. It also means that the authors used various literary tools such as metaphor, parables, poetry, story and hyperbole to express their message. Understanding the literary form of a particular text is essential to grasping its full meaning.

In my reflections throughout this book, I have relied upon the writings of mainline Protestant and Catholic scholars (see Bibliography) for their historical and cultural analysis along with over 40 years of personal experience as a minister of God's Word. Just as the various Biblical authors shared their faith experience formed from the fabric of their historical and cultural lives, this book represents my Catholic upbringing in the 50s, my ideological formation during the turbulent 60s, my 22 years as a priest, and 23 years as a husband and grandfather.

Each unit is followed by two questions to facilitate the integration of the material. This text is not to be read in the fashion of a book, but masticated each day as food for the soul. Because any reading of the Scriptures is filtered through our personal background, I began this journey with a series of meditations on the Divine images that have impacted our spirituality.

DIVINE IMAGES

March 7, 1958, I was preparing my bag lunch breakfast of peanut butter and jelly sandwiches when I unconsciously licked the knife. I immediately realized the horror of my mistake. "How can I possibly go to communion now that I broke my fast?" I continued to contemplate my dilemma when I arrived at church for morning Mass. The obvious choice would have been to avoid going to communion, but this was the Lenten season and also a first Friday, which meant that everyone chose to receive the sacrament. If I were to remain in my pew while everyone else went forward, they would think that I had committed a grievous (mortal) sin. You can imagine what thoughts would have been percolating concerning this 14-year-old adolescent, even though I didn't do anything wrong. If I chose to go to communion, I would have committed a serious sin for violating the required fast. My choice came down to remaining in the pew and letting my peers think of me as a sinner, or committing a sin by going to communion but keeping my reputation intact. I chose the latter.

I knew I could go to confession the next day and relieve myself of this sinful burden. Unfortunately, when Saturday came we had some unexpected visitors, so I was not able to see a priest to relieve myself of the guilt I carried. On Sunday morning I was faced with the same family dilemma. Everyone went to communion, so I couldn't possibly stay in the pew and let them wonder about the son who was planning to go to the seminary in the fall. Once again I chose to receive communion, thus committing a sacrilege. I was now on the fast track to hell. I continued to go to Mass every day the following week and throughout the Lenten season, maintaining my perfect record for daily communion and intensifying the fires that would greet me when I died.

Since I was so steeped in sin, I was too ashamed to confess to the local priests. Even though we were afforded the anonymity of the confessional, I knew they knew my voice. How could someone who was planning to study for the priesthood become such a degenerate?

Compounding my sinfulness, I was chosen among all of those who received communion daily during Lent to crown Mary on May 1st. It was a special honor and a privilege. On May 1st, I climbed the ladder carrying the crown of roses with trembling hands as the choir sang "On This Day O Beautiful Mother." I remember telling her how sorry I was, and that I didn't mean for it to go this far, while anticipating a lightning bolt striking me dead. I was never so scared in my life. It wasn't until I went to confession to a priest in the seminary that I finally felt the terrible burden of guilt and sinfulness lifted from my soul.

This story reveals an image of God that was internalized and operative in my psyche during my formative years. In this chapter, I will be reflecting on the various metaphors of God and how they impact our understanding about spirituality, politics, economics and gender.

Reflection:

1. What religious practices impacted your formative years?
2. What image of God did these reflect?

DIVINE PUNISHER OR COMPASSIONATE SAVIOR

Throughout the scriptures, whenever God or an angel encounters someone, the first words spoken are: "Do not be afraid." Such an expression is easy for God to say, but the human recipient is challenged to decide whether he/she is meeting the Divine Punisher or the Compassionate Savior. Both descriptions of God are in constant tension throughout the entire Bible.

In Genesis we are told that the Creator became so disgusted with everything after Adam and Eve ate the forbidden fruit that He decided to destroy the earth and everything on it except for Noah, his family and the various pairs of animals. Such a solution obviously failed, since humankind continued to rebel by building the Tower of Babel. However, the Divine Punisher continued "His" rampage against sinful humanity with the destruction of Sodom and Gomorrah, saving Lot and his family, but turning Lot's wife into a pillar of salt for peeking at the devastation.

When the Israelites were wandering in the desert living on manna and water day after day, they complained against God and Moses, so the Lord sent poisonous snakes to teach them a lesson (Nm. 21: 6). When they began cavorting with Midianite women, the Divine Punisher sent a plague that killed 24,000 (Nm. 25:6-9). After Moses led the people for forty years and put up with their rebellious attitude and constant complaints, the Divine Punisher forbade him to enter the promised land, citing his lack of faith when he struck the water-giving rock twice instead of once as commanded (Nm. 20:11-12).

When the Israelites entered the Promised Land under Joshua, God ordered them to kill every man, woman and child living in the cities they captured. In the battle at Gibeon, the Lord killed more of the Amorites with hailstones than the Israelites did with swords (Josh. 10: 11).

In establishing penalties for various sins, the Divine Punisher made it clear that the laws were to be taken seriously. Anyone who had sex with his stepmother, daughter-in-law or neighbor's wife needed to die. Any man who slept with another man had to be executed. If a man married a woman and her mother, they were to be burned to death. Any man or woman who had sex with an animal would be killed along with the animal (Lv. 20). If a parent had an unruly teenager, or one who was a glutton or drunkard, they needed to report him to the city elders who would have him stoned to death (Dt. 21: 18-21).

The Divine Punisher made it clear that disobedience to sacred laws involved severe penalties: "The Lord will strike you with Egyptian boils and with tumors, eczema and the itch, until you cannot be cured. And the Lord will strike you with madness, blindness and panic so that even at midday you will grope like a blind man" (Dt. 28:27-29).

The theme of the Divine Punisher is found throughout the Hebrew Bible in the books of the Prophets, Daniel and Psalms. It continues in the New Testament culminating in the final destruction of Satan and all unbelievers in the battle of Armageddon.

Juxtaposed to the Divine Punisher is the image of Compassionate Savior, a concurrent theme throughout the Scriptures. In Genesis, the Creator fashions us into the Divine image, looks at all creation and declares it to be "very good." In Exodus, the Compassionate Savior "sees the suffering of his people and hears their cries." The legal codes of Leviticus and Numbers reveal a God obsessed with justice for those without any status in a Patriarchal system: the widow, orphan and the alien. The prophets, as Divine spokesmen, demand social justice as an expression of authentic worship.

Jesus is the ultimate revelation of the Compassionate Savior. When asked by Peter how often we need to forgive, he responded: "seventy times seven" (Mt. 18:22), meaning we must always be willing to forgive. He taught us to love our enemies, pray for those who persecute us and to respond non-violently to violence (Mt. 5:38-45, Lk. 6:27-35). He died forgiving His persecutors.

John the Baptist firmly believed in a God of retribution (Lk. 3:7-9). When he was in jail, he sent his disciple to see if Jesus was really the expected one because of the reports he'd heard. Jesus responded by saying: "The blind regain their sight, the lame walk, lepers are cleansed, the deaf hear, the dead are raised, the poor have the good news proclaimed to them. And blessed is the one who takes no offense at me" (Lk. 7: 22-23). In other words, I have not come to punish, but to heal.

What is the true character of God, the Divine Punisher or the Compassionate Savior?

If Jesus is the full revelation of the Father, could it be that the image of the Divine Punisher is simply a projection reflecting the Patriarchal culture of power and control?

If Jesus reveals God as the non-violent one, could it be that the Divine cleanup of this world expressed in gory detail (Rev. 14:20, 19:17-21) is a projection of an oppressed people longing for vengeance?

If Jesus reveals the heart of God on Calvary, could it be that our history of turning the cross into a sword reflects our unwillingness to accept such a vulnerable Savior? Could it be that we are far more comfortable with the weapons of power than the cross of surrender? Could it be that we have created God into our own image and likeness?

Do not be afraid reflects the heart of a Compassionate Savior, not the attitude of a Divine Punisher.

Reflection:

1. Divine Punisher or Compassionate Savior—how has the tension between these two images impacted your spiritual journey?

2. How do these two images continue to evoke differing understandings of Judaism, Christianity and Islam?

THE LAWGIVER/JUDGE

"Happy are those...who walk by the teaching of the Lord who observe God's decrees."(Ps. 119:1-2). In the Jewish tradition, the covenant on Mt. Sinai (Ex. 19) resulted in the great gift of the law. The 613 commands expressed God's expectations for the people and were seen as a source of happiness.

In the Christian tradition, emphasis on the law was determined by the cultural differences between the Eastern and Western church. Eastern theologians were more speculative and mystical in their thinking. "God became human so that we may learn how to become God" (Clement of Alexandria and Athanasius). Spirituality was the process of discovering the God within. Western theologians were more practical. They had to deal with the great influx of barbarian tribes. They adopted the Ten Commandments (Ex. 20:1-17) as the basis for spirituality and a means of establishing a semblance of social order among their new converts. As a result, the Western fathers focused on morality as the foundation of religion, and the image of God as Lawgiver/Judge became the dominant metaphor. It was the Western tradition that influenced our understanding of religion to our present day.

According to the spirituality of morality, God, the Lawgiver and Judge, demands strict obedience to his laws and punishes violators according to the severity of their crimes. In the Catholic tradition, anything to do with sex, missing mass on Sunday or eating a hot dog on a Friday resulted in damnation if not confessed with proper sorrow, a firm purpose of amendment and doing the required penance. Every commandment was analyzed so that you knew what acts were considered mortal (resulting in eternal fire if not confessed) or venial (just a temporary scorching in Purgatory). Despite its obvious flaws, the system offered a certain sense of security, because one's performance was the barometer of his/her spirituality. You either broke one of the commandments or you didn't.

Unfortunately, we usually responded to God out of fear rather than love. Obeying rules became more important than embracing grace. Religion was a merit system on how to earn our way to heaven rather than a response to the good news of God's unconditional love in transforming this world.

This type of religion impacted our spirituality in several ways. First of all, it created numerous people like Luther, who before his conversion wallowed in his guilt and sinfulness. Secondly, it satisfied many of our ego needs: the need to be right, morally superior and self-righteous. "I accepted Jesus as my Lord and Savior." "I worship weekly, say my prayers and read my bible daily." "I fast, tithe, abstain from alcohol and never use offensive language." We tended to focus on our external behaviors rather than our inner motivations. While we admitted our sins, we denied the real area that needed to be addressed and transformed. Finally, it emphasized personal salvation at the expense of social consciousness. We focused on our private failings and remained ignorant of the systemic evil that perpetuates economic injustice, racism, sexism, consumerism and violence.

The key to God's covenant with Israel on Mt. Sinai was the relation-ship, not the laws. When laws overshadow the relationship, religion becomes a reward and punishment system in which we try to prove ourselves to a demanding judge rather than surrendering ourselves to an unrelenting lover.

Reflection:

1. What are the pros and cons of the Ten Commandments?

2. Lawgiver or Lover: How do these images impact social consciousness?

KING

The politics of power and control have impacted the Judeo-Christian discourse since the time of pharaoh. Under this arrangement, all power was in the hands of the wealthy elite, the top 10% who con-trolled the political, military and economic structures of their day. Because of their wealth, they were able to manage the populace by writing the laws of governing and establishing the economic and tax policies that secured their investments.

The whole system was justified with religious underpinnings that declared pharaoh or the king as a divinely chosen ruler. Loyalty and obedience to the ruler expressed submission to the deities.

In the Exodus experience, God offered the Israelites a whole new vision of reality. The escape from Egypt was more than a journey from slavery to freedom; it was a transition from the politics of exploitation to the economics of justice. The legal codes found in Exodus (20:22-23:19), Deuteronomy (12-16) and Leviticus (17-26) established fiscal policies that challenged the prevailing politics of inequality.

Unfortunately, this radical experiment reflecting God's vision for humanity came to an end after 250 years because of the need to have a centralized authority to deal with the internal and external pressures that threatened to destroy the tribal alliances. Once the people demanded a king like other nations, many of the Biblical texts began to describe God as a distant all-powerful monarch, ruler, warrior, lawgiver and judge. Israel soon reverted to the power and control system they experienced in Egypt. However, the prophets and Jesus maintained the tradition that God's kingship was like that of a compassionate shepherd who hears the cries of the oppressed and continues to subvert the existing social structures in order to create a more just society.

The image of God as an all-powerful king greatly impacted the history of Christianity. For the first 300 years when the church gradually developed a hierarchical structure (pope, bishops, deacons) the primary metaphor for God was Jesus as the good shepherd. However, once Christianity became the state religion of Rome under the emperor Constantine, church leaders adopted the clothing and trappings of power reflecting their exalted status, and the institutional structure mirrored the Roman system.

One could argue the merits of this evolution, but when Rome fell to the barbarians in 476, the papacy stepped in to fill the leadership vacuum and restore order to society. The transition helped preserve Western civilization, but it also created an environment for religious leaders to become trapped in their own version of the power and control system.

The tension between the image of God as imperial monarch protecting our sacred institutions and the compassionate shepherd calling for their transformation will remain with us until the end of time. Emphasis on the metaphor of divine monarch creates social stability. Emphasis on the compassionate shepherd invites ongoing conversion and passion for those devalued by society. Unfortunately, history has demonstrated that religious and civil leaders have been more interested in preserving their institutions and maintaining control rather than caring for their people.

Jesus understood the meaning of systemic evil as he experienced how the religious and political institutions of his day exploited the people. His passion for God's kingdom led him to oppose those systems, and it cost him his life. His call to discipleship is an invitation for each of us to do what we can to transform our little worlds.

Reflection:

1. How does the King metaphor continue to dominate our political and religious discourse?

2. What is your understanding of strength and weakness?

MALE

From the time we were children we learned to address God as our Father. The masculine imagery became so ingrained in us that we simply accepted the male metaphors as being totally expressive of the divine nature. It never occurred to us that those images have profound consequences socially, politically and sexually. We didn't understand that the scriptural metaphors of King, Lord and Warrior reflected the ancient patriarchal systems of the Middle East and the Greco-Roman culture. The imagery not only expressed those structures, but also justified them. Just as the Divine King ruled the heavens, His male representatives governed the earth, perpetuating the myth of female inferiority.

However, the biblical texts also express a counter-cultural tradition that reveals the feminine side of God as a nurturing mother, wise woman and one giving birth. The first chapter of Genesis reminds us that we were created male and female in the Divine image. Unfortunately, many religious teachers throughout history have ignored this text and focused on the creation of Eve from the side of Adam (actually a sign of equality) as a proof text of her inferiority. They have also used the story of Paradise lost to show that Eve, the first sinner, is a model of feminine seduction.

The ministry of Jesus demonstrated openness to women that defied the cultural norms of his day. He had a special friendship with Martha and Mary reflected in his comfort of staying at their home. He had several women disciples who followed him from Galilee to the cross and became witnesses of his suffering and death because the apostles all ran for their lives. The woman at the well who had five husbands became his apostle to the Samaritans. Mary Magdalene, the leader of the women disciples, was the first to witness the resurrection. Jesus clearly accepted women as co-workers in his ministry.

The letters attributed to Paul reveal an ambiguity about the status of women. In Galatians (3:28), women and men are equal by virtue of their baptism, but Ephesians (5:22-23) tells women to be submissive to their husbands who rule the household. Paul ends his letter to the Romans by sending greetings to a number of men and women who are his co-workers in Christ, including Junia, a female relative called to be an **apostle** before him. He also recommends Phoebe, a **deacon** of the church at Cenchreae. However, the first letter to the Corinthians (1Cor. 14:34-35) contains a later insert telling women to remain silent in church, and the letter to Timothy states that women are not to teach men (1 Tm. 2:2-12). The timeline of these letters indicates that as the church became more institutionalized it adapted the patriarchal culture of society, thus reducing the role of women in ministry.

The tension between the patriarchal system favoring men and a more egalitarian system that accepted the role of women in numerous ministries continued for the first few centuries as evidenced by the writing of a number of church fathers. Tertullian (an early third century theologian) quotes the precepts of ecclesiastical discipline concerning women to address a situation in northern Africa.[3] "It is not permitted for a woman to speak in the church; but neither (is it permitted for her) to teach, nor to baptize, nor to offer the Eucharist, not to claim for herself a share in any masculine function, and not to mention any priestly office."[4] He cites a law written to eliminate practices once considered normative in some communities. There is evidence to indicate that women were functioning in sacerdotal roles until the end of the fifth century. "We have heard that divine things have undergone such contempt that women are encouraged to serve at sacred altars, and that all tasks entrusted to the service of men are performed by a sex for which these (tasks) are not appropriate" (Pope Gelasius writing to bishops in southern Italy).

History is always written from the viewpoint of the winners or the established system. This also applies to the church, which justifies its teachings, its ministry and its hierarchical/patriarchal structure as divinely ordained. Since God is male, it is only fitting that men who reflect the divine image should govern and minister. However, many of the Protestant traditions have since adopted a more egalitarian approach to ministry by allowing women to pastor and preside at worship.

The male imagery for God also impacts our liturgical texts. The constant use of masculine pronouns (he, his) perpetuates our male bias and the generic term "men" for all humans continues to devalue women.

The ongoing use of masculine metaphors to describe the divine source of life profoundly altars our consciousness, our understanding of gender roles and our belief in the way reality is ordered. Today, numerous women throughout the world continue to be victimized by violence, control and domination because they are considered inferior by their male counterparts. We must never underestimate the power of language and imagery.

Reflection:

1. How has the male imagery influenced your understanding of God?

2. How does a male-only clergy impact women?

FACES OF THE CREATOR

The bible tells us that we are made in the image and likeness of God. Unfortunately, most of us spend our whole life living out of a false sense of self. Instead of acting out of our identity as God's sons and daughters, we have become trapped in our ego needs to be somebody based on religious, ethnic, political, economic or personal characteristics. As long as we continue to live life on this level, we will perpetuate the divisions that tear us apart.

Jesus defied the purity and holiness codes of his day by reaching out to those rejected by society. As his followers, we need to see the face of the Creator within the faces of those who are different from us. Just as Francis of Assisi became liberated when he embraced a leper, we will break the chains that bind us when we reach out in love to all our brothers and sisters, regardless of their status in society.

Who are these people we are called to embrace?

The little old lady devoid of memory staring blankly at the wall and muttering incoherently.

The veteran with shrapnel in his brain frightened by his memories and the cauldron of rage boiling within.

The billionaire CEO who lives with the illusion he is a self-made man who has it all.

The bishop who has spent his life serving the church at the cost of losing his humanity.

The single mother struggling to make ends meet, hoping just to get through another day.

The young woman longing for love and acceptance, exposing herself to multiple sexual partners.

The old derelict smelling of urine and grasping his bottle of comfort.

The young man who just acknowledged his sexual identity, but remains petrified that others may learn his secret.

The elderly woman facing death without the support of family or friends.

The young couple whose lives were shattered with the sudden death of their child.

The faithful Muslim despised for his religion and feared as a potential terrorist.

The many politicians either trapped in their rigid ideologies, or those willing to say or do anything to get elected.

The multiple faces of ethnic diversity that have become the focus of racial profiling and political scapegoating.

The aging actress desperately trying to cling to her youthful appearance.

And you and I as we look at ourselves in the mirror each morning.

We are all the face of the Creator. Mother Teresa often doubted the existence of God, but was able to sense the divine presence in a fly-covered person left to die on the streets of Calcutta. Jesus taught us to see beyond the superficial and embrace divinity at the heart of our humanity. "For I was hungry and you gave me food; I was thirsty and you gave me drink; a stranger and you welcomed me; naked and you clothed me; ill and you cared for me; in prison and you visited me" (Mt. 25:35-36).

Reflection:

1. Who are the lepers in your life?
2. What does it mean for you to be an image of the Creator?

THE GOD I DON'T BELIEVE IN

When I was growing up, God was like a cruel Santa Claus who not only kept track of whether we were naughty or nice, but he replaced the chunk of coal in the stocking with eternal damnation for such terrible crimes as missing mass on a Sunday or eating a cheeseburger on a Friday. For lesser crimes we would be tortured with scorching fire until our debt was paid: a process known as purgation. I no longer believe in such a sadistic Divinity.

I don't believe in the God who destroyed just about every living creature with a flood, and then decided to let us regenerate with the same flaws as our predecessors. I don't believe in the God who dictates laws condemning adulterers, homosexuals, fortune tellers and unruly teenagers to death (Lv. 20). I don't believe in the tribal God of the early Israelites who ordered them to kill all of the captive Midianites (men, women and children) except the virgins (Nm. 31:13-18). I don't believe in the control freak who forbade Moses entrance into the Promised Land for striking the water-giving rock twice instead of once (Nm. 20:7-13). I don't believe in a God who wills the death of innocent people in a "just" or "holy" war (crusade or jihad).

I don't believe in a God who claims that the only way to salvation is to accept Jesus as a personal Lord and savior, even if it means that Jews, Muslims, Hindus and any other non-Christian person is excluded. I don't believe in the God imbedded in our psyches as a white male and used to justify the suppression of women and minorities throughout history.

The male metaphor is only valid if balanced with the female imagery, because both genders are made into the image and likeness of the Creator (Gn. 1:27). The ethnic metaphor undermines our common humanity when universalized. Finally, I do not believe in a God who required his pound of flesh by demanding his son die in order to save us sinful creatures. The theology of substitutionary atonement is only one of several interpretations for Jesus' life and death.

The fact of the matter is that I do not believe in the God reflected in most of our preaching and piety, because the images portrayed are usually a projection of our own fears and concerns. In effect, we have created an idol of ourselves.

The God I believe in is beyond our comprehension and cannot be expressed with our limited language. Our words, rituals and art can only offer glimpses into the Divine mystery.

I do believe in a Trinitarian God who reminds us that all of creation is relational and connected, thus exposing the fallacy of dualistic thinking which divides us from one another and justifies the exploitation of our natural resources. I do believe in a God who is the life force within all of creation and desires the fullness of life for all of us. Therefore, I firmly believe that when we are diminished or marginalized in any manner, God enters into our pain with compassion, desiring justice and liberation. The Biblical texts offer multiple examples. "I have witnessed   the misery of my people... I have come down to rescue them" (Ex. 3:7).

I do believe in a God who is more concerned with social justice than public worship, (Is. 1:16-17; Amos 5:24). I do believe in a God who is less concerned about private piety than our response to those in need (Is. 58:6-8; Mt., 25:31-46). I do believe in a God who identifies with those who suffer from economic and political exploitation. "He who oppresses the poor blasphemes his Maker" (Prov. 14:31).

I believe that God's vision for us was manifested through the life of Jesus. I believe that the Spirit of God empowers us to participate in the ongoing transformation of this world. I believe the cross is the cost of discipleship and the resurrection expresses God's ultimate "yes" to our humanity. Finally, whether we accept it or not, I do believe that God's final judgment is "I love you."

Reflection:

1. What God do you believe in?

2. Why is it so difficult to have a meaningful discussion about God?

FORMATION OF A PEOPLE

The primal experience of God in the Scriptures was as Liberator, not Creator. The Exodus narrative begins with a new Pharaoh "who knew nothing of Joseph" (Ex. 1:8). Scholars are unable to determine the identity of this Egyptian potentate who embarked on an ambitious building project around thirteen hundred years prior to the Christian era.

According to the narrative, the new Pharaoh was a harsh taskmaster, demanding increased production from his slaves to build more supply cities (Ex. 1:1-11) to house all of his grain. He oversaw the daily operation, pushing his foremen to make sure his subjects continued to meet their daily quotas of brick-making while forcing them to find their own straw (Ex. 5:4-19).

Egypt was the super power of the Middle East, controlling numerous city-states who paid significant taxes for protection. The socio-economic system placed Pharaoh at the top of the pyramid as a divine king. Those who supported him and helped administer the government became wealthy off the backs of the working class and poor. The military provided protection and enforced the unjust policies. The gods were worshipped to guarantee their ongoing blessings of power and wealth.

At the time of the Exodus, Israel did not exist as a people. The term "Habiri" referred to those considered outside the law and who often created problems for the individual city-states. Archeologists have uncovered a number of letters from various subject kings written to Pharaoh requesting help to subdue these dissident groups. It is unclear if the term refers to the origin of the Hebrew people. What is certain is that the group that left Egypt was of mixed ancestry (Ex. 12:38).

The Exodus experience began with the people giving voice to their agony. The pain of oppression touched the compassionate heart of the Divine Liberator. "I have witnessed the affliction of my people....I have come down to rescue them" (Ex. 3:7-8). God then recruited Moses and Aaron as the human agents to bring the plan to fruition.

The pursuing struggles between Moses and Pharaoh reflected the battle between the gods of Egyptian oppression and Yahweh, the Liberator. Although the outcome was never in question, the Egyptians were able to match Yahweh's Divine power for the first two plagues. After the third plague, the all-powerful Pharaoh began to sense that his illusory world was falling apart. In an attempt to maintain some semblance of control, he began to negotiate with Moses and Aaron. He granted them permission to go and worship their God, provided they not go too far away. He even asked for their prayers (Ex. 8:24). Then he tried to maintain control over their animals, but that also failed (Ex. 10:24). ⁵ He finally submitted to the inevitable and asked them to bring a blessing upon him by their leaving. (Ex. 12:31-32). Led by Moses and Aaron, this diverse group of oppressed people began their long trek from slavery to freedom.

The story of Exodus is the archetype for all those enslaved by ruthless pharaohs who continue to become wealthy off the backs of the working class and exert their power over others while fearing the demise of their position. The pain of agony can be heard today from those struggling to live on a minimum wage as they cry out against the pharaohs of fast food chains and multi-billion dollar retailers. The pain of agony can be heard from the many women devalued monetarily, sexually and intellectually as they cry out against the male pharaohs who fear gender equality. The pain of agony can be heard from those physically, emotionally and spiritually assaulted by the pharaohs of their religions. The pain of agony can be heard from the parents of Columbine, Newtown and countless other cities as they cry out against the pharaohs who control the gun lobby. The pain of agony can be heard from the environment as it cries out for justice against the pharaohs who exploit the land, the sea and the sky.

God continues to hear the cries of those oppressed and recruits new Mosaic leaders: Pope Francis, the first pope from the Americas who proclaims a gospel of compassion and inclusiveness to those enslaved by religious righteousness; Bishop Tutu, a leader against apartheid who continues to teach the value of non-violence and forgiveness to a world trapped in a never-ending cycle of violence and revenge; Malala Yousafzai, a 14-year-old girl who survived a Taliban bullet to her head, yet continues her campaign to educate women enslaved by ignorance; and Rev. Mary Raymerman, a convert to Catholicism who defied ecclesiastical sanctions to become one of the first American women ordained to the priesthood, leading the way for others to break the barriers of an all-male clergy.

Listen! The Divine Liberator is also calling you.

Reflection:

1. Who are the Pharaohs in your life?
2. What is your calling at this stage in your life?

WILDERNESS

"Would that we had meat for food! We remember the fish we use to eat without cost in Egypt, and the cucumbers, the melons, the leeks, the onions and the garlic. But now we are famished; we see nothing before us but this manna" (Nm. 11:4-6).

The journey from slavery to freedom always begins with great elation until confronted with the reality of entering into the unknown. Once the discordant group of slaves experienced the harsh realities of the desert, they began to question the wisdom of leaving the security of Egypt. "Would that we had died by the Lord's hand…as we sat by our fleshpots and ate our fill of bread! But you had to lead us into this desert to make the whole community die of famine" Ex. 16:3).

The forty year journey was not only a process of becoming free, but the development of a community. In order to survive the harsh conditions of the barren environment, this group of quarrelsome nobodies gradually learned the importance of cooperation. The wilderness not only represents a geographical location, but the psycho-social experience of exile and chaos manifested in the constant complaints and rebellion of the people. It also reveals God's gratuitous response to their many demands in the form of water, quail and manna.

Unfortunately, the wilderness is very real for thousands of people displaced by war, violence, oppression and terrorism. Numerous children risk their lives daily crossing through deadly environments in their attempt to enter our borders. Millions have left the wars in Iraq and Syria to settle for the inhumane conditions of refugee camps. Hundreds risk their lives crossing dangerous seas in search of a new life. Imagine their desperation and fear!

The sojourn through the desert captures the human experience of becoming free. Like the Israelites, we are all enslaved to something: addictions, ignorance, fear, ideology and unhealthy relationships, but the journey to freedom demands that we leave the security of what we know to enter into the unknown. This is why we are always tempted to return to our old patterns of living. Even though we know deep inside that our present condition will never free us to experience life more fully, we often choose to remain in our comfort zone. We see this happen with many addicted to drugs or alcohol as they relapse after coming out of treatment. Abused spouses often return to the violence from which they escaped because of the fear of facing life alone. It is safer to cling to our secure belief systems than question those policies that conflict with our experience.

Like the Israelites, we are better at complaining than living in the moment. We are often anxious about the next day, week or month. We become so blinded by what we consider negative experiences that we fail to see the wonder of life unfolding around us. We constantly complain about government, religion, people, expenses, sickness and weather so much so that we fail to fully appreciate God's daily manna in the form of those who love us, the health to do what we do, food on our tables, a roof over our heads, the beauty of a sunrise or the sounds of nature.

Despite the many complaints, the Divine Liberator continues to bless our journey to the Promised Land. Just as the wilderness transformed a group of nomadic slaves into the Israelites, it also transforms us into God's intended people.

Reflection:

1. What has been your experience of wilderness?
2. Why is the wilderness necessary for building community?

COVENANT

When the newly freed band of slaves arrived at Mt. Sinai, they encountered their Divine Liberator. Unlike the gods of Egypt, God chose to enter into a special relationship with this discordant band of runaways if they would obey the Ten Commands laid out by Moses. The core of this fundamental Decalogue demanded a total surrender to the Redeeming Deity and a commitment of love and respect for each other. This relationship was clearly summed up in the two great commandments of loving God and neighbor. Moses ratified the covenant when he sprinkled the blood of a young bull, first on the altar signifying God, and then on the people who responded: "All that the Lord has said we will heed and do" (Ex. 24: 6-8). It is clear from the Book of Deuteronomy that the covenant was conditioned on the response of the people: blessings for obedience; curses for dis-obedience (Dt. 11:26-28).

As the people reflected on this newly formed relationship, they began to understand that the Divine Liberator was presenting a totally new socio-economic vision of reality. Unlike the gods of Egypt that simply blessed the hierarchical political model, their God demanded an egalitarian prototype based on distributive justice where everyone could benefit from the resources available. The Divine Liberator became an economist, defending the rights of the widows, orphans, aliens and the poor—all those without rights in the patriarchal society of the Middle East.

The first law of the Divine Economist was the Sabbath rest. "Remember to keep holy the Sabbath day. Six days you may labor and do all your work, but the seventh day is the Sabbath of the Lord, your God… the Lord made the heavens and the earth, the sea and all that is in them, but on the seventh day he rested" (Ex. 20:8-11).

"The idea that every seventh day must be set aside as sacred rest is distinctively and uniquely Jewish"[6]. The motive expressed in Exodus is an imitation of God's respite after six days of creating. The reasoning in Deuteronomy (5:12-15) was a reminder that the Israelites were once slaves in Egypt and had to work seven days a week. The Sabbath rest forced the rich and the poor to live as equals for at least one day a week. It was a temporary reprieve from the daily experience of inequality. [7]

The principle of Sabbath rest was then extended to a year. "For six years you shall sow your land and gather in its produce but on the seventh year you shall let the land lie untilled and unharvested , so that the poor among you may eat" (Ex 23:10-11 and Lv. 24:2b-7). These laws remind us that even the land belongs to God and deserves a rest to regenerate itself. A corollary to these laws was the provision for the poor who also have a right to the land and its produce. [8]"When you reap your harvest in your field and overlook a sheaf there, you shall not go back to get it; let it be for the alien, the orphan and the widow" (Dt. 24:19-21,Lv.19:9-10). The second economic law was the forbidding of loans with interest to fellow Israelites. "When one of your countrymen is reduced to poverty and has to hold out beside you, extend to him the privileges of an alien or a tenant, so that he may continue to live with you …Do not exact interest…You are to lend him neither money at interest nor food at profit. (Lv. 25:35-37, see also Ex. 22:25 and Dt. 23:19).

The third policy was the remission of debts. In the Book of Deuteronomy, the seven-year rest was also transformed into a time to remit all debts (Dt. 15:1-2, 7-11). The remission of debt also applied to slavery, the most extreme form of indebtedness. Exodus (21:7-11) and Deuteronomy (15:12-15, 18) made provision for the freeing of those who sold themselves into slavery to pay off their debts.[9]

The final law was the Jubilee year. It occurred every fifty years and required that all land be returned to the original owners. "This fiftieth year you shall make sacred by proclaiming liberty in the land for all its inhabitants. It shall be a jubilee for you, when every one of you shall return to his own property, everyone to his own family estate" (Lv. 25:10). "The land shall not be sold in perpetuity for the land is mine, and you are but aliens who have become my tenants" (Lv. 25:23). The purpose of the law was to prevent the small family farms from being taken over by greedy landowners. The fundamental principle underlying these laws is that our God is passionate about justice.

The prophetic tradition explicitly states that authentic worship of God demands fairness. Any ritual that ignores the widow, the orphan and the alien is empty and an abomination to the God of Justice (Read Am. 4:1-5,5:21-24; Is. 1:10-17; Mi. 6:6-8; Jer. 7:5-7). The theme of economic justice is also expressed in numerous psalms, various proverbs and the book of Job (29:12-17).

These laws were established for an agrarian economy, and reflect a rejection of the patriarchal system the Israelites experienced in Egypt. They were designed to maintain an egalitarian structure that prevented a few wealthy people from exercising all of the power and controlling the resources. [10] It is apparent from the prophetic literature that most of these laws were ignored once Israel, to be like the other nations, chose a king.

The principles underlying these legal codes continue to challenge everything we hold sacred in a capitalist system. They undermine our need for constant acquisition. They unmask the falsehood of fair competition. They expose the myth that poverty is due primarily to personal laziness rather than systemic injustice. They debunk the "trickle down" theory of economics, because greed will always supersede the common good. They are a searing reminder that the Creator is the owner of all that we have. They expose our relationship with God by revealing our true attitudes to those most in need.

In today's political milieu, God would be labeled a socialist or Marxist for defying the divine dictates of unbridled capitalism. It always amazes me that throughout history we have shifted the focus from God's desire for distributive justice to Divine wrath over sexual peccadillos when the preponderance of concern throughout the Bible is economic not pelvic.

Reflection:

1. What are the economic implications of loving God and neighbor?

2. What are the positive and negative results of our capitalist system?

PROMISED LAND

The Joshua narrative offers a glimpse into the formation of the Hebrew Bible. According to the logic of the preceding books, this text should be included in the Torah: Genesis, Exodus, Leviticus, Numbers and Deuteronomy. Following the pre-historical stories (Gn. 1-11) ending with the tower of Babel, the Torah continues with the promise of land to Abraham. Joshua tells the story of obtaining their sacred inheritance. The priestly school of editors who composed the final draft removed it from its logical location because the Jews were exiled at the time in Babylon and did not occupy their promised real estate.[11]

The Book of Joshua justifies Israel's claim to the Promised Land, remaining a source of contention to this very day. The narrative describes the occupation as a swift conquest of the indigenous Canaanites. Archeological and historical evidence suggests that the process was far more complex.

The land was composed of numerous city-states that operated according to the same socio-economic paradigm as Egypt. The kings and city-elites heavily taxed the rural peasants in exchange for military protection. Once the Israelites established a foothold in the hill region around Shechem, word began to spread about the God of Liberation who demanded an egalitarian socio-economic form of governance. This led to an internal revolt in a number of the city-states, while others peacefully integrated through alliances and intermarriage. The gradual process of occupation was a combination of Israelite conquest, internal rebellion and assimilation.

The text describes a liturgical celebration where new members were initiated into the community by proclaiming their belief in Yahweh and embracing the egalitarian system of the Israelites. "Put away the strange gods that are among you and turn your hearts to the Lord, the God of Israel" (Josh. 24:23). As their numbers increased, the people were gradually divided into twelve tribal units. The new members shared stories of their patriarchal ancestry. These were incorporated into the national history, beginning with the call and promise to Abraham, a further justification for claiming the land as their rightful inheritance.

The book of Joshua presents a major theological problem. The first twelve chapters describe the military conquest and portray the Divine Liberator as a god of violence who demands the total destruction of every man, woman and child (Josh. 10:34-40).

The text justifies the use of violence against indigenous people for real estate entitlement. It justifies the current policy of Jews against Palestinians. It justified our violent policies against Native Americans to claim our "promised land." It has been used to justify the Spanish conquest of the Aztec and Mayan peoples, and European colonialism throughout the world. It continues to provide a religious excuse for justifying violence against our perceived enemies.

We cannot ignore the fact that Joshua is part of our sacred heritage. It is my personal belief that the narrative represents a more primitive state of our human consciousness. As the revelation of a compassionate and non-violent God in numerous other sacred texts permeates our awareness, we are gradually awakening to a deeper understanding of the Divine Liberator.

Reflection:

1. How can we justify the Book of Joshua or other violent texts as being part of God's inspired Word?

2. Why do we continue to glorify violence?

TWO CONTRASTING COVENANTS

The Hebrew Bible reflects the ongoing tension between two differing models of governance: charismatic-egalitarian and hierarchical-institutional. The differences are expressed in the covenant God established with Moses and the Israelites on Mt. Sinai (Ex. 20, 24:6-8), and the one established with David in Jerusalem (2 Sm. 8:-17). The first covenant created a total regime change; the second reestablished the domination system of Egypt.

The history of Christianity reveals this same conflict. Paul's letters show that as the church became more institutional, it developed the patriarchal values of society. When it became the religion of Rome, it adopted all the trappings of power and the empirical form of governing.

During the feudal system, a person's economic and social status expressed God's will. The pope and king stood at the top of the ecclesiastical and political pyramids. All authority flowed downward, requiring total obedience from those deemed socially inferior.

At the beginning of the 15th century, the church was in a quandary because there were three competing popes. Reacting to this dilemma, a number of bishops attempted to reduce the power of the papacy with the authority of a council. The Counciliar movement was short-lived, but it awakened a longing for a more democratic form of governance realized in some segments of the Protestant Reformation. The invention of the printing press in1450 began the dismantling of the Catholic Christian theocracy. As literacy increased the centralized power of the church gradually began to decrease.

The Age of Enlightenment gave birth to democracy, including freedom of worship and freedom of speech. The Catholic Church reacted with anathemas and the doctrine of papal infallibility. The First Vatican

Council reflected the fear of growing secularism by reiterating the hierarchical understanding of the church with the emphasis on clerical leadership. Pius X followed by requiring all clergy to take an oath against Modernism.

The Second Vatican Council expressed a more egalitarian ecclesiology (People of God) in dialogue with secular society, and called all baptized to utilize their gifts to create a better world. Trying to regain centralized control of a "runaway" church, John Paul II and Benedict XVI attempted to roll back the clock. Francis has refocused the energy from orthodoxy and legalism to inclusiveness and compassion. He is attempting to decentralize the Vatican influence and restore the power of the regional bishops' conferences.

Both covenants are most effective working in tandem. Kings Hezekiah (715-686 B.C.E.) and Josiah (640-609 B.C.E.) exercised royal power while remaining faithful to the Moses/Sinai covenant. The spirit-led egalitarian form of governance cannot withstand internal and external pressures before disintegrating. The hierarchical model of centralized power stagnates over time when the charisms of the people are ignored or repressed. Perhaps one day we will learn to live within the paradox of the charismatic/egalitarian and institutional/hierarchical forms of governance without fighting the temptation to choose one or the other.

Reflection:

1. What are the strengths and weaknesses of the two covenant systems?

2. How does our representative form of government reflect or negate our democratic values?

ISRAEL ESTABLISHES A MONARCHY

"The elders came to Samuel and said to him, 'Now that you are old, and your sons do not follow your example, appoint a king over us, as other nations have, to judge us.' Samuel was displeased with their request and prayed to the Lord, who responded: 'It is not you they reject; they are rejecting me as their king'" (1 Sm. 8:4-7).

The Books of Samuel express Israel's radical transformation from a loosely organized confederation of tribes to a centralized state. A number of factors influenced this transition: the threat of the Philistines, who monopolized the market of iron weaponry, the development of urban centers of power, the accumulation of wealth and the struggle for land.

The elders recognized that the old order was not working. Israel was no longer able to deal with the external threat of its enemies and the internal tensions between the tribes. Their request for a monarchy was a rejection of their religious foundation. They chose the security of a political system with its military backing over the inscrutable manner in which Yahweh had guided them for the past 250 years (Book of Judges). Reluctantly, God granted the request, but told Samuel to warn them about the consequences of their decision.

Samuel's speech is a critique of the abuse of power that came to be the norm in Israel under the monarchical system. [12] "The king will take your sons and assign them to his chariots and horses, and they will run before his chariot... He will set them to do his plowing and his harvesting, and to make his implements of war and the equipment of his chariots. He will use your daughters as ointment-makers, as cooks and as bakers. He will take the best of your fields, vineyards and olive groves, and give them to his officials. He will tithe your crops and your vineyard, and give the revenue to his eunuchs and his slaves. He will take your male and female servants as well as your best oxen and use them to do his work. He will tithe your flocks and you yourselves will become his slaves" (1 Sm. 8:11-17). Israel would truly become "like the other nations" with all the power and control in the hands of the wealthy elite.

The account of Saul's reign is the tragic story of a heroic leader trapped in the transitional period between the collapse of the old Tribal Confederacy represented by Samuel, and the birth of a new social order established by David.

The conflict with Samuel came to a head in the victory over the Amalekites when Saul was ordered to totally destroy everyone and everything. Saul failed to carry out the ban by capturing the king and saving the best of the sheep and oxen. His disobedience cost him Yahweh's support. "I regret having made Saul king, for he has turned from me and has not kept my command" (1Sm. 15:11).

Since Saul was no longer Yahweh's king, God told Samuel to go to Bethlehem to anoint one of Jesse's sons as the new king. Because this was an obvious act of treason, Samuel was instructed to pretend his purpose was to offer sacrifice (1Sm. 16:2).

The rise of David parallels the decline of Saul. As a warrior and leader, the multi-talented shepherd boy overshadowed the increasingly jealous Saul, whose paranoia was aggravated by David's personal charm, gallantry and success. In Saul's mind all of David's actions were designed to claim the throne. Although David remained totally faithful to his king, Saul became obsessed with hunting him down and killing him. Confronted with forces beyond his understanding, Saul became increasingly unstable and eventually died on a field of battle by falling on his own sword in the midst of defeat (1Sm.31:4).

When God allowed Israel to choose a king, the king was to remain obedient to the covenant commands of justice. The Divine hand was at work despite all the political intrigue, the numerous battles, the family disputes, sexual seduction and attempted coups.

God entered human history in a very unique manner at the time of the Exodus. The covenant flowing from that encounter challenged the Israelites to organize a society based on total obedience to their Savior and respect for all their members, especially the poor, the widows, orphans and aliens. The new monarchy was to continue the tradition of revealing to the nations how a God-centered society functioned.

The heart of the Sinai covenant was the people's relationship with God reflected in their association with each other. That primary premise remains valid after 3,000 years. As a Christian people, we are called to love God with our whole heart, soul and strength (Dt.

6:5), and our neighbor as ourselves (Lv. 19:18), regardless of the political and economic systems in which we live.

Reflection:

1. Where do you see God's hand at work amidst the political, cultural and religious turmoil in our society?

2. What does our modern-day conflicts between religious or secular conservatives and liberals say about who we are as a people?

KING DAVID

The transition from a federation of tribes to a centralized nation was completed under the leadership of David. His rise to power (2 Sm. 1-8) demonstrated his military and political genius. David began to build his power base while serving as a mercenary army leader for the king of Gath by protecting the southern tribes from Philistine attacks. He was crowned King of Judah shortly after Saul's death, and ruled from Hebron for seven years while he patiently waited and outmaneuvered Saul's surviving son to win over the loyalty of the northern tribes.

After David captured Jerusalem from the Jebusites, he made it his capital. Since the city was independent of the old federation, he was able to establish his government free of all tribal claims.

As he gained the loyalty of all of Israel, he reorganized the army and defeated the Philistines who had provided him safety during his years as an outlaw. He extended the borders from the "river in Egypt to the Euphrates" in fulfillment to the promise made to Abraham (Gen. 15:18, Jos. 1:4).

In order to underpin his authority with religious sanctions and to assuage the fear that his political innovations were destroying the ancient traditions, David brought the Ark of the Covenant, which symbolized Yahweh's presence, from Shiloh to Jerusalem. In effect, he shifted the religious center from the tribal sanctuary to the royal shrine in Jerusalem. He placed the Ark in the Tent of the Meeting (Ex. 40:34), thus joining together the two major cultic objects inherited from Mosaic times (2 Sm. 7:2).

The Lord validated David's rule in one of the most important passages of the Hebrew Bible. When David requested Nathan's guidance concerning his desire to build a temple to house the Ark, God's response through the prophet was a new covenant that validated the royal social order. "I will establish a house for you... I will raise up your heir after you, sprung from your loins, and I will make his kingdom firm forever. I will be a father to him, and he shall be a son to me... I will not withdraw my favor from him as I withdrew it from your predecessor Saul. Your house and your kingdom shall endure forever before me; your throne shall stand firm forever" (2 Sm. 7:12,15-16).

Unlike the Moses/Sinai covenant (Ex. 20-24) that was conditioned upon Israel's obedience to the law, the Davidic covenant was unconditional. Yahweh's gift to David was pure grace. "It was I who took you from the pasture and from the care of the flock to be commander of my people Israel. I have been with you wherever you went, and I have destroyed all your enemies before you" (2 Sm 7:8-9).

The new covenant with David ratified a historical/political reality. It was as much royal propaganda as an expression of faith in God's inscrutable ways. It provided a foundation for Israel's hope during times of subjugation and exile. It also gave rise to the belief that God would one day send another messiah like David who would reestablish His Divine rule.[13] However, in the view of many, the Davidic covenant did not replace the Moses/Sinai agreement, and the tension between the two is expressed through much of the Old Testament. Similar conflicts exist between state and federal governments, and hierarchical and egalitarian ecclesiologies.

The Court History (2 Sm. 9-1; Kgs. 2) reveals the dark side of royal power. David's forced labor gangs (2 Sm. 20) and establishment of a military draft (2 Sm. 24) became hated elements of his administration. David was able to conquer all of his external foes and heal the national wounds with the family of Saul, but was unable to keep peace in his own family. His adultery with Bathsheba, and cover-up resulting in the death of her husband, Uriah the Hittite, was a blatant abuse of authority. Although he repented when confronted by the prophet Nathan, God passed a judgment upon his house. "I will bring evil upon you out of your own house" (2 Sm. 12:10-11). David's son Amon raped his half-sister Tamar and was slain by his brother Absolom. David spared Absolom, who then planned a coup to take over the throne, but was killed by David's general Joab. In his old age, another son, Adonijah, tried to take over the throne, but was stopped by Nathan and Zadok, the priest. The Court History reads like a soap opera, but it shows again that despite all the intrigue and plotting, God's hand was at work. Although David and his successors were far from perfect, the Lord remained faithful to the royal covenant for four hundred years.[14]

Despite his failings, David so captured the imagination of the Israelite people that future generations looked to him for inspiration. As an outlaw running from King Saul, he gathered together a group of the socially marginalized and inspired hope among generations of outcasts. As a sinner he accepted responsibility for his actions and humbly acknowledged his penance. He gave expression to national grief over the deaths of Saul and Jonathan (2 Sm. 19-27), and demonstrated a father's agony over the killing of his rebel son Absolom (2 Sm. 19:1-1-5). The author of Chronicles was inspired by his piety and accredited him with organizing Israel into a worshipping community. The Book of Psalms is attributed to his authorship reflecting the community's belief that David was the ideal king and the prototype of the coming King, who would fulfill the hopes of Israel. As a ruler, he knew the limits of his power: a lesson many of our modern leaders have yet to learn.

Reflection:

1. What are the qualities of a great leader?

2. Why do you think David became idealized more than Moses?

SOLOMON: ROYAL WISDOM AND DIVINE FOOLISHNESS

The beginning of the First Book of Kings continues the drama known as the Court History. Who was going to succeed David: Adonijah, the eldest son and logical choice, or Solomon, son of Bathsheba? The text tells us that David was in a weakened state suffering from poor circulation. The once powerful ruler, who demonstrated his virility with multiple wives and concubines, needed a virgin simply to help keep him warm. "The king did not have relations with her" (1 Kgs. 4) was a euphemistic way of saying he was totally impotent.

Nathan, the prophet, hatched a successful plot to deceive David into thinking he swore an oath to Bathsheba that her son would be his successor. Solomon was declared king, and he quickly eliminated all his enemies in accordance with his father's advice.

The picture of Solomon in chapters 3-10 is one of faithful obedience to the God of Israel. When the Lord appeared in a dream and promised to grant whatever he wished, the new king asked for the wisdom to govern. The gift was granted, and Solomon became one of the most influential rulers in the Middle East.

Solomon married Pharaoh's daughter and instituted the Egyptian model of government. Since it was a time of peace, he was able to launch into multiple building projects. He built a luxurious palace, a wall around Jerusalem, and fortified his military outpost. The temple, considered one of the wonders of the Middle East, became his most famous project. Building the temple fulfilled David's dream and centralized all worship. It provided a guarantee of God's presence and gave rise to the hope that one day the Lord would rule over all of creation and establish a program of peace and justice. The text tells us that when the queen of Sheba saw all that Solomon accomplished, it took her breath away (1 Kgs. 10:5).

Solomon's reign reflected a time of peace and prosperity unknown in Israel's history. From all external evidence, he was by far the most successful of all the kings. His wealth, international alliances, harem, arms trade and success of his work projects revealed a man of power, political acumen, administrative skill and financial genius.

However, the Deuteronomic authors considered Solomon a dismal failure. The son who began with such great promise was ultimately seduced by the power of his office. The once obedient servant of Yahweh lost his heart to his foreign wives and their gods that he also worshipped. He conscripted many of Israel's sons into the army and forced others into labor camps. He raised taxes to pay for bigger government, and he intentionally redistricted the old tribal boundaries to reduce their influence. His abuse of power planted the seeds that led to a national schism shortly after his son became king. The northern region became Israel and the southern territory became Judah.[15]

The Book of Kings demonstrates the ongoing tension between the Mosaic and Davidic covenants. The northern kingdom, consisting of ten tribes, remained rooted in the Moses/Sinai tradition despite several attempts to establish royal dynasties. Lacking a strong centralized government, they were unable to fend off the Assyrians who destroyed the Nation in 722 (BCE). The draconian policy of exporting most of the people and intermingling those remaining with groups imported from other countries created a people of mixed ancestry known as the Samaritans.

The southern kingdom was able to survive another 150 years because of the centralized system of governance rooted in the Davidic covenant and dynasty. However, in 587 (BCE) the Babylonians destroyed any illusions of perpetuity when they leveled Jerusalem, the temple and monarchy, and forced the leading citizens into exile.

The Deuteronomists completed their work during the Babylonian exile around 550 (BCE). The sources they cited in their text included the Acts of Solomon, The Chronicles of the Kings of Judah, and the Chronicles of the Kings of Israel.[16] Reading these sources, a person without faith would easily conclude that Israel's decline was the result of incompetence, miscalculation and ill-advised treaties.

The authors of Kings believed both kingdoms were destroyed because of their disobedience. They viewed history through the theological lens of the Mosaic/Sinai covenant: obedience equals blessings; disobedience equals curses. Later theologians would challenge the simplicity of that belief (Book of Job) and present other explanations for evil, such as the presence of Satan expressed in the Books of Daniel and Revelation.

The Deuteronomic history, covering Joshua, Judges, Samuel and Kings, proclaims God as active in the social, economic and political climate of the times. The Lord of history can utilize the most unseemly characters and circumstances to accomplish the Divine plan. These books remind us that the kingdom is not just some heavenly dream, but an earthly reality gradually unfolding as our human consciousness develops in accordance with God's will.

Could it be that God used Ronald Reagan, Pope John Paul II and Michel Gorbachev to bring about the downfall of the Soviet empire? Could it be that God was able to use the senseless violence in Northern Ireland to bring about the Good Friday Peace Agreement? Could it be that the mindless killing of innocent people is now being used to turn the Muslim world against Al Qaeda and Isis? Could it be that God is using our economic interdependence to raise our consciousness as a global family? Could it be that our negative reaction to thousands of refugees is forcing us to examine our national values and identity? Could it be that our personal sinfulness is the gateway to God's transforming grace? Could it be?

Reflection:

    1. Who are today's Solomons?

    2. How has God used your personal turmoil?

PROPHETIC CHALLENGE
TO ROYAL POWER

The prophet was a spokesman for God and the people. As an Israelite, his identity lay fully and completely with his people, but as one called by God, his vocation was to be an emissary of the Divine Word. Caught between the people he loved and the message of judgment he had to render, the true prophet lived a life of agony. The prophets were not so much prognosticators as truth tellers.

Once the Jewish people requested a king of their own, God sent prophets to critique the use of that power in light of the Mosaic or Davidic covenants. They were not radical liberals pushing a progressive agenda, but conservative traditionalists who understood that social justice was the human expression of God's nature. Fidelity to Yahweh demanded sharing resources with the poor and outcast of society. The prophetic voices confronting the abuse of power and unjust economic policies paralleled the history of the monarchy.

"The task of the prophetic ministry was to nurture, nourish and evoke a consciousness and perception alternative to the consciousness and perception of the dominant culture around us"[17].They needed to break through the conventional wisdom and present a vision of reality viewed from God's perspective.

In our lifetime, Martin Luther King, Jr. used the Exodus imagery to stimulate the civil rights movement of the Sixties. The Berrigan brothers employed prophetic actions to challenge the wisdom of the Vietnam War.

In the booming prosperity of the northern kingdom under Jeroboam II, the prophet Amos (760 B.C.E.) challenged the commercial transactions that created the widening discrepancy between rich and poor (Am. 2:6-8, 5:7,10-12, 8:4-7). He did not speak in generalities about being charitable. His indictments pointed to specific practices used to defraud the peasants.

The relentless drumbeat for social justice extended for 250 years until the end of the monarchy. Hosea (12:7-9), Isaiah (3:14-15), Micah (2:2; 3:1-3), Jeremiah (22:3, 13, 15-17), Ezekiel (45:9-12) and Zechariah (7:9-10) reflect God's consistent demand that his covenant with the people (Mosaic) and the king (Davidic) not be ignored or mocked.

Amos (4:1, 4-5; 5:21-24), Isaiah (1:10-17), Micah (6:6-8), Jeremiah (7:5-7, 9-11) also challenged any ritual divorced from social justice. They condemned the elaborate liturgies that were devoid of expression in everyday living. Ritual without reality was meaningless.

The prophets were also radical monotheists. They interpreted the first commandment of the Decalogue (Ten Commandments) in its strictest sense. Religious freedom was not to be tolerated. The king and people were to worship only the God who freed them from Egyptian slavery. Just as the prophets challenged unjust economic policies, they decried political alliances with other nations because of the influence of their foreign gods.

The demands of faith took precedence over security needs. This was clearly demonstrated in the confrontation between Isaiah and Ahaz. When the kings of Israel and Aram surrounded Jerusalem,"the heart of the people and the heart of the king trembled as the trees in the forest" (Is. 7:2). Isaiah's message was simple: Do nothing. Trust the Lord. When the king and people feared an Assyrian attack, they made a futile alliance with Egypt. God responded, "by waiting and by calm you shall be saved; in quiet and in trust your strength lies. But this you did not wish" (Is. 30:15).

There were many in Israel who claimed a prophetic ministry, but lacked the insight into God's will and the reality of sin. They identified the national agenda as the Divine plan. In contrast, the Biblical prophets proclaimed a Heavenly revolution that would transform the entire nation. The God who created the national institutions was capable of dismantling them in order to create something new.

Believing themselves to be God's chosen people, the Israelites turned a deaf ear to the messengers. They held a privileged status among the nations of the world and a theology that gradually domesticated God. They believed it was in God's best interests and reputation to sustain and bring prosperity to the nation and protect their sacred institutions: Jerusalem, temple and monarchy.

Israel's great sin was to confuse the gift with the Giver. The official theologians, false prophets and priests firmly believed that a God powerful enough to create a people from slavery was powerful enough to sustain them. Israel may have been unfaithful, untrue and undeserving, but God was always faithful and true. The call to repentance and efforts at reformation were human attempts to manipulate God into sustaining the Divine gifts. The real prophets, who were considered false in their day, also called the people to repentance, but understood that reformations were ultimately illusory. They believed in God's radical freedom and were able to distinguish the Giver from the gifts. The God who brought the people out of Egypt could also bring them out of Palestine. The God who gave them the land, the sacred city, the temple and the king could also take them away. They understood that Israel's true mission was to live totally dependent upon the God who could create newness out of nothingness.[18] "I will give you a new heart and place a new spirit within you, taking from your bodies your stony hearts" (Ez. 36:26); and from Jeremiah, "I will make a new covenant with the house of Israel and Judah... I will place my law within them and write it upon their hearts. They will no longer need someone to teach them to know the Lord" (Jer. 31:31,33).

Although the prophets were ignored, rejected or assassinated, their voices continue to speak to us today; their message of radical monotheism forces us to look at the many gods we have created to provide us with security; their message of social justice challenges the prevailing greed of our economic system; their message of God's radical freedom undermines the false confidence we place in our religious and civil institutions; their message of transformation challenges us to let go of our attempts to manage and control our lives; and their message reminds us that God is not an American, Catholic,

Baptist or Lutheran. God is not even a Christian. God is God, and any domesticating beliefs are a false teaching.

Reflection:

1. How can one discern a false prophet from a true prophet in our own time?

2. How have we as a nation and as individuals domesticated God for our own purposes?

ELIJAH AND ELISHA

Throughout the two Books of Kings, the Deuteronomic authors grade the various monarchs of the northern and southern kingdoms according to their ability to unite royal power (David) with covenant obedience (Moses). In the midst of their analysis, they suddenly inject the prophetic alternative to royal propaganda (1 Kgs. 17:1ff) as demonstrated by Elijah and his disciple Elisha. The text reveals how the spirit of God empowered Elijah to save a gentile woman and her son from starvation (1Kgs. 17:7-16), raise a widow's dead son to life (1Kgs. 17:17-24) and single- handedly confront 450 prophets of Baal, the fertility god (1Kgs. 18:19-40).

After defeating the prophets of Baal, Elijah escaped the clutches of the vindictive Queen Jezebel. Symbolically repeating the Exodus experience, he wandered in the desert forty days and nights, returning to the source of Israel's faith on Mt. Horeb/Sinai where he encountered God, who commissioned a regime change. The Divine Liberator did not communicate through the powerful forces of nature, identified as gods: wind, earthquake or fire, but the sound of a gentle whisper (1Kgs. 19:1-18).

The Elijah cycle ends with him giving a double portion of his spirit to his disciple before ascending into heaven (2Kgs. 2:11). His return is anticipated every year during the Passover meal where a place is set in his honor.

The Elisha cycle continues the same remarkable demonstration of Divine power: he rescues a poor widow who was about to lose her children to unscrupulous creditors (2Kgs. 4:1-7); he promises a son to a barren mother and gives life to her offspring after he dies (2Kgs. 4:8-37); he heals a Syrian general of leprosy (2Kgs. 5:1-19); he feeds a starving community by turning a scarcity of food into abundance (2Kgs. 5:42-44); he negotiates a peace by commanding his king to feed their Syrian enemies with a bountiful banquet (2Kgs. 6:13a-23), and he provides food during a time of famine from the supplies their enemies abandoned (2Kgs. 7:6-18).

The Elijah and Elisha stories are often dismissed as folklore. Walter Brueggemann, the renowned scripture scholar, argues the intent is to demonstrate an alternative experience of reality. Royal power is limited by what it can control: the kings cannot fertilize a barren womb; the kings cannot create abundance from scarcity; the kings cannot produce rain during droughts; the kings cannot cure leprosy; the kings cannot bring lasting peace through war; and the kings cannot/resuscitate the dead. Filled with the Spirit of God, the two prophets have the power to bring about the seemingly impossible— the Spirit blows where it wills, defying logic, reason and predictable patterns. [19]

The Elisha cycle begins and ends with two metaphorical stories. When Elisha starts his ministry, he is mocked by a group of boys: "Go up bald head... Go up bald head!" (2Kgs. 2:23-24). When he cursed them for their ridicule, two she-bears came out of the woods and tore forty-two of them to pieces. This rather gory episode reminds us that God's word, incarnated in the prophet, will not be scorned. In the second story, a band of Moabites threw a dead man into Elisha's grave. When the deceased touched the bones of the prophet, he came back to life (2Kgs. 13:20-21). The prophet may be dead, but his life-giving spirit lives on.[20]

Just as Elijah and Elisha manifested an alternative consciousness to royal power, Jesus, Peter and Paul captured the imagination of the people with their challenge to imperial authority. "The blind see, the lame walk, lepers are cleansed, the deaf hear, the dead are raised, and the poor have the good news proclaimed to them" (Lk. 7:22). They paid with their lives.

God's truth has been released by human agents throughout history, creating an alternative storyline to the status quo. Francis of Assisi, Luther, John XXIII, Mahatma Gandhi and thousands of others have lifted the veil of perceived normalcy and revealed the possibility for newness. "You cannot imprison the word of the Lord"[21] (2Tm. 2:9).

Reflection:

1. Where is God's alternative reality being manifested?

2. How have our civil and religious institutions attempted to imprison the word of God?

AMOS: PROPHET OF SOCIAL JUSTICE

Amos came from the small village of Tekoa about ten miles south of Jerusalem. In addition to being a shepherd, he was a dresser of sycamore trees. The fruit of the sycamore was the diet of the poor. While unripe, it had to be punctured to help it ripen to an edible state. His job allowed him direct contact with the plight of the underprivileged.[22] From the quality of his poetry and the masterful way in which he handled words, it would seem that he was either educated or especially gifted. Like all of the prophets, Amos had an awareness of international politics and alliances.

At the time of his calling, the Hebrews were divided into two nations. Israel was comprised of the northern tribes, while Judah was united with the tribe of Benjamin. The two kingdoms were politically, economically and militarily independent, but they shared the same religious beliefs. Amos was a southerner called by God to preach to the leaders and people of the northern empire.

He ministered during the reign of Jeroboam II (750 BCE). It was a time of peace and great prosperity. Unfortunately, the economic boom resulted in social upheaval. The peasants and farmers, who had been the backbone of the nation, now found themselves oppressed by the greedy nobility. Poor people were dispossessed of their small plots to form larger agri-businesses. Their appeals landed on the deaf ears of judges corrupted by bribes. The wealthy believed God rewarded their lifestyles because the prevailing theology proclaimed blessings on those faithful to the covenant.

Religious devotion and liturgy flourished in the midst of this adulteration of the Mosaic covenant. The sanctuary at Bethel was filled to overflowing with worshippers offering expensive gifts and sacrifices. Formalism in ritual characterized the religion of Israel. Few people seemed to care that the dehumanizing lot of the poor was in direct conflict with the faith they professed.

It was Amos' firm contention that Israel had been chosen by God to have a special responsibility to the peoples of the world. Israel's vocation was one of service, not privilege. He decried the irresponsibility of the rich in forming a social pyramid. Class distinction was destroying the covenanted-community and was bringing doom upon God's people.

In a crude style reminiscent of Elijah, he decried the obscene opulence of some of the wealthy women: "Hear this word… you cows of Bashan, you who oppress the weak and abuse the needy… They shall drag you away with… fishhooks" (Am. 4:1-2). Needless to say, many husbands endured scorched ears that evening.

The Book of Amos ends with a series of visions concerning the impending destruction of Israel. The "Day of the Lord" had been anticipated by the people as a time when the Lord would secure victory for Israel over her foes. Amos viewed this "Day" as a time of judgment, because Israel had forgotten the social implications of their Mosaic faith.

When Amos challenged the religious hypocrisy of the day, the high priest Amaziah denounced him to King Jeroboam as a conspirator against the government. Like any true prophet, Amos confronted the complacent religious fraud that divorced piety from life. As a result, he was driven from the country.

God's word spoken through Amos continues to inspire and challenge us today: "I hate; I spurn your feasts; I take no pleasure in your solemnities. Your cereal offerings I will not accept… Away with your noisy songs! I will not listen to the melodies of your harps. But if you would offer me holocausts, then let justice surge like water, and goodness like an unfailing stream" (Amos 5: 21-24).

Reflection:

1. There are over 2000 verses in the Bible dealing with the poor and God's response to injustice. Why have our religious institutions failed to address economic issues?

2. What is the purpose of our prosperity?

HOSEA: PROPHET OF DIVINE LOVE

Hosea's ministry covered a period of some 26 years (c. 750-724 BCE). His work began during the reign of Jeroboam II when Amos prophesized. The kingdom was fractured between those who were pro Egyptian and those who favored an alliance with Assyria. Since the people in the northern kingdom were not formed by the David/Jerusalem covenant, the monarchy did not have the theological underpinnings that supported the dynasty of the southern kingdom as evidenced by the murder of four kings during his ministry.

Hosea has the distinction of being the only writing prophet from the northern kingdom. He was more cosmopolitan than Amos, and his pronouncements revealed a deep sensitivity for the plight of the people. [23]

Both Amos and Hosea were grounded in the Mosaic covenant emphasizing social justice. Whereas Amos projected the personality of a stern and austere shepherd, Hosea personified the loving kindness that he preached. He was a prophet deeply in love with the people he felt obliged to condemn. Like a loving father, he experienced the conflicting emotions of one who must punish an erring child.

Hosea viewed the Moses/Sinai covenant as a marriage between God and the People. His keen insight into God's love came from his own experience with Gomer, his unfaithful wife. Despite her repeated infidelity, Hosea remained committed and continuously offered forgiveness and the opportunity to begin anew. He understood that his relationship with Gomer reflected God's limitless love for the people despite their continuous whoring after other gods.

When the Israelites settled into the Promised Land they adopted some of the practices of the Canaanite culture, including the worship of Baal, the god of fertility. Although the Israelites accepted God as their Liberator, they weren't sure about Yahweh's ability to control the agricultural cycles. Hosea was absolute in his demand that sole and total allegiance be given to Yahweh, who delivered them from bondage. For people who made a living off of the land, such an idea was extremely radical and dangerous.

Hosea demanded allegiance to God, who was totally committed to the people. The Hebrew word "hesed" describes a relationship that is faithful, kind, tender, loving and forgiving. It is a type of love that is passionate beyond words. Hosea challenged the people to know God in this deep personal manner, just as God expressed "hesed" for them.[24]

Despite Hosea's constant appeals for the people to return to the Lord, much like his wife, they chose not to listen. The Israelites continued in their ways, trusting in foreign alliances, military force and the fertility gods. For Hosea, this was the root of Israel's sin: relying on anyone or anything other than the God who chose them. Chapter eleven reveals the deep pain of a parent who loves his rebellious child and is forced to punish her in the hope that she will eventually reciprocate. "When Israel was a child I loved him, out of Egypt I called my son… I fostered them like one who raises an infant to his cheeks… They did not know that I was their healer… My heart is overwhelmed, my pity is stirred. I will not give vent to my blazing anger."

Hosea understood that Assyria would be the instrument of God's punishment. When Israel refused to pay tribute, the Assyrians attacked and destroyed the northern kingdom (722 BCE). A number of citizens were able to escape to the southern kingdom along with their written traditions. Some of these, such as Hosea's prophecies and a section of the Book of Deuteronomy, were eventually incorporated into the Old Testament.

As was their practice, the Assyrians scattered the leading citizens to other parts of the empire for the purpose of breaking any geographical, cultural and religious bonds of national identity and loyalty. Foreigners were brought into Israel to mix with those left behind, and eventually formed a people known as the Samaritans.

The northern tribes were never heard from again, but the words of the prophet continue to echo through the ages. "For it is love I desire, not sacrifice, and knowledge of God rather than holocausts" (Hosea: 6:6).

Reflection:

1. Who are the gods we worship as individuals and as a country?

2. Hosea states that the people violated the covenant because they did not know God. Knowledge in Hebrew is an act of the heart. What have your relationships taught you about God?

ISAIAH: PROPHET OF UNWAVERING TRUST

The Book of the Prophet Isaiah is divided into three major sections. This reflection will focus on Isaiah's ministry from 740 until 690 (BCE) contained in Chapters 1-39. Chapters 40-55 reflect the writings of a prophet who ministered during the Babylonian exile (586-538 BCE). Chapters 56-66 reproduce prophecies written after the exile until about 400 (BCE).

Isaiah was born in Jerusalem in 760. He was a contemporary of Amos, Hosea and Micah. We know that he was married and had as least one son. Unlike his northern counterparts, Isaiah was influenced by the royal theology of the southern kingdom (2 Sam. 7).

The message of Isaiah can best be understood in the context of his call (Is 6:1-13). During a Temple visit, he had a vision of Yahweh enthroned and surrounded by the Celestial Court. Isaiah was overcome by terror and a sense of his own human sinfulness. Transformed by the encounter, he offered his life to Yahweh as to a king who commands total allegiance. As God's emissary, he would continuously demand the same loyalty from the people.

Like Amos, Hosea and Micah, Isaiah attacked social corruption and the oppression of the poor. He condemned the luxury-loving women of Jerusalem, the land-grabbers, the skeptics, the self-sufficient and those who perverted justice.

Isaiah's teachings also contained elements of promise. He developed the doctrine of a remnant, predicting that the small group of people who remained faithful to God's Word would become the cornerstone of a new Israel (Is.10:20-21). He also foresaw a time when the nation would be ruled by an ideal king (Is. 9:5-6, 11:1-9). Early Christians used these texts in their understanding of Jesus as the expected messiah.

Isaiah had to face three major crises during his ministry. The first occurred when the northern kingdom and Syria tried to force Ahaz, the king of Judah, to enter into an alliance against Assyria. Isaiah tried to convince Ahaz to do nothing and that God would take care of it. "The virgin shall be with child and bear a son, and shall name him Immanuel" (Is. 7:14). This sign indicated that God was with the people and would bring about the defeat of their enemies. The king failed to listen and formed a coalition with Assyria, sparing Judah, but surrendering the people's faith for a foreign religion, symbolized by the pagan altar erected in the temple.

The second crisis occurred during the reign of Ahaz's son, Hezekiah. Egypt sought to stem the power of Assyria by urging an alliance of the Palestinian states in exchange for military aid. Hezekiah was under a great deal of pressure to join the coalition. Isaiah dramatically advised against it by walking naked for three years through the streets of Jerusalem as a living symbol of the disgraceful exile that would result should they trust the Egyptian promises of aid (Is. 20:2-5). Once again he emphasized that neither human cleverness nor diplomacy would protect Judah. God alone would provide the necessary support for the nation.

The final crisis occurred when a new ruler came to power in Assyria. In 702, Sennacherib's army moved down the Mediterranean coast destroying the members of the coalition. Although Judah was devastated, Jerusalem was spared and some small vestige of independence was preserved, but only because Hezekiah bought off Sennacherib at a terrible cost. Once again, the king resorted to human means of deliverance[25].

Although the citizens of Jerusalem were saved, Isaiah believed that they had sold their souls to preserve their lives. In what may have been his final oracle, he appears to reject his own traditions as he announces the destruction of the city (Is. 22:1-8). The behavior of the king and people nullified the Davidic/Jerusalem covenant. Ironically, because the sacred city and the temple were spared, the people developed the irrational belief that they were inviolable.

Isaiah's oracles are complex, containing judgments as harsh and strident as Amos combined with visions of a transformed future that rival Hosea. He offered elements of condemnation, challenge and promise that were treasured by later generations as they encountered life and death decisions.

Reflection:

1. Picture yourself as Kings Ahaz or Hezekiah. Your city is under siege, and Isaiah tells you do nothing, but trust in God. What would be your reaction?

2. How would Isaiah address our present climate of fear?

JEREMIAH: PROPHETIC AGONY

"Before I formed you in the womb, I knew you; before you were born I dedicated you; a prophet to the nations I appointed you… This day I set you over nations and over kingdoms, to root up and to tear down, to destroy and to demolish, to build and to plant"(Jer.1:5,10).

During the final years of Judah's independence, God's call came to a teenager named Jeremiah. His prophetic activity spans from 626 to 580 (BCE). By the end of his career, Jerusalem lay in ruins and the People of God were captive exiles in Babylon.

Judah was a small nation that managed to survive as a vassal state under Assyrian and Egyptian rule. The fact that Jerusalem, the Temple and the Davidic Dynasty survived the onslaught of various armies reinforced the prevailing belief that God remained faithful to the Davidic Covenant. These divinely sanctioned institutions would never be destroyed.

Jeremiah's mission was to proclaim an end to the dynasty, the city and the temple. Even though he felt deeply committed to his Lord, Jeremiah was not a willing prophet like Isaiah. Throughout his ministry he wished he had never been called to such a miserable vocation. He agonized over the horrible things he had to announce. "The corpses of the people will be food for the birds of the sky and beasts of the field... In the streets of Jerusalem I will silence the cry of joy, the cry of gladness... for the land will be turned to rubble" (Jer.7:34).

Telling the people that God had chosen Babylon as the instrument of Divine Judgment, Jeremiah had been prophesying disaster for over 25 years. His predictions went unfulfilled. King Jehoiakim treated his prophecies with contempt. When Jeremiah's secretary, Baruch, read the prophet's warnings to the king, he cut off each section of the scroll and burnt it in a fire (Jer.36:23). Others took him more seriously: they beat him, threw him into a cistern and attempted to kill him. Jeremiah was enraged by this treatment and confused at the apparent injustice of God who allowed his servant to suffer while his enemies prospered. His confessions (12:1-5; 15:10-21, 17:14-18; 18:19-23; 20:7-18) are intense personal prayers that reveal the agony of his interior life. "Cursed be the day on which I was born! May the day my mother gave me birth never be blest" (Jer. 20:14)! Sensitive and reflective, he did not hesitate to inform the Lord about his personal pain in carrying out his mission. "You duped me, oh Lord, and I let myself be duped; you were too strong for me and you triumphed. All day long I am an object of laughter; everyone mocks me..." (20:7). God's word was like a fire burning within his heart and bones overpowering his attempts to hold it in. Despite the constant derision, it was less painful and tiring to speak the designated oracles. Jeremiah's prayers ranged from violent outbursts of anger and cries for vengeance to proclamations of confidence and praise. He was a man torn apart by the terror of his vocation and his love of God, who called him to be a prophet.

In 598, Jeremiah's prophecy began to be fulfilled when the Babylonians captured the city. Many of the leading citizens were taken into exile and a puppet king was placed on the throne.

King Zedekiah was a good man but a weak ruler, who did not have the strength to resist the influence of the anti-Babylonian nationalists. When he refused to pay the required tribute, the Babylonians returned with a vengeance and destroyed the city, the temple and the dynasty. They placed a governor over the land and took more of the leading citizens into exile. They granted Jeremiah the freedom of a collaborator.

After the destruction of the sacred institutions, Jeremiah became a prophet of hope. He wrote to those in exile and told them that they would remain in Babylon for 70 years, but that God was using their experience to purify them. He expressed the radical notion that God was not confined to the Promised Land, but was present with those in exile. He also proclaimed a new covenant: "I will place my law within them and write it upon their hearts; I will be their God and they shall be my people" (31:33). They would no longer have to rely on fallible preachers and teachers to communicate knowledge of the Lord.

After a group of radical nationalists murdered the proxy governor, they forced Jeremiah to go with them to Egypt. He ended his days separated from the land and the city that would be reborn when his people returned from exile. According to legend he was murdered by those he was called to serve. Jeremiah's sufferings, born of the love he had for the Lord and his people, became a major contribution to the history of our faith. His life may have inspired the suffering servant oracles of the exilic prophet known as Second Isaiah (Is. 38-56), and revealed the unspeakable pain in the heart of God.

Reflection:

1. Have you ever had the experience of being seduced by God?

2. What institutions do we consider sacred and inviolable?

Ezekiel: Prophet of Divine Judgment and Promise

The writings and actions (Chapters 3,4,5,12) of Ezekiel reflect a fertile imagination and a profound sense of drama. The son of a priest, born and raised in Jerusalem, he rose to prominence among the aristocracy and was among the first taken into exile by the Babylonians, who deported the nation's leaders as a means to subdue the people.[26] Unlike the Assyrian policy of scattering conquered people throughout the Middle East, the Babylonians allowed the people of Judah to settle in roughly the same area, making it possible to maintain a communal life.

Unlike most of the previous prophets who communicated verbally, Ezekiel was a brilliant literary artist who conveyed God's word through his writings. He used grandiose and fantastic symbols facilitating the birth of later apocalyptic literature such as found in the Book of Revelation.

He received his call to be a prophet in 593(BCE) by means of an extraordinary vision (Ez. 1:4-28) revealing God as dynamic, mobile, all-knowing and transcendent. Ezekiel's initial task was to convince the people that God would demolish Jerusalem and the temple, and join them in exile. The sacred institutions needed to be destroyed because the people failed to fulfill their covenant responsibility. Convinced that God would never allow such a thing to happen, Ezekiel found his prophecies falling on deaf ears. Many believed that the city and temple were inviolable because of the Davidic covenant.

Ezekiel's wife, the "joy of his eyes," died in 587, and her death became the medium of the Lord's most disturbing message. Unable to speak of her death because the pain was beyond words, he went into shock. His loss and reaction symbolized the fulfillment of God's word. Like the prophet, the exiles were forced to grieve the unspeakable death of their country and their shattered belief in God's covenant.

In the aftermath of the destruction, Ezekiel was called to be a watchman, responsible not only to the community in general, but for each individual. He challenged the prevailing notion that the sins of the fathers were visited upon the sons when he introduced the radical notion of individual responsibility within the larger community.

Reflecting on the reasons for such terrible events, Ezekiel condemned the upper classes for the unjust manner in which they treated the people of inferior status (Ex.34:1-7). He also criticized those at the bottom of the socio-economic system for the violence inflicted on each other (Ez.34:17-22). Such horizontal violence is frequently the only outlet for the frustration and helplessness among the dispossessed.

Ezekiel used the most graphic language to describe the long history of Israel's infidelity. "She is a whore who spreads her legs for all those who pass by: the Egyptians, Assyrians and Babylonians" (16:25, 23:20). The greatest tragedy of 587 was the profanation of God's reputation among the nations. Yahweh expected the people to reveal the Divine Nature as merciful, forgiving, compassionate and kind. Unfortunately, their behavior was so bad that God was forced to uproot them from their land. After several decades, the banishment was rescinded.

"Not for your sake do I act, house of Israel, but for the sake of my holy name, which you profaned among the nations… Thus the nations shall know that I am the Lord… when I prove my holiness through you… I will take you away from among the nations… and bring you back to your own land… I will give you a new heart and place a new spirit within you, taking from your bodies your stony hearts and giving you natural hearts" (Ez. 36:22-26).

In another dramatic revelation, Ezekiel envisioned God birthing life from death. The nation of Judah would be resuscitated as illustrated by the dry bones being transformed into living bodies (Ez. 37:1-14). Later generations reflected on this vision as foundational for their belief in an afterlife.

Visualizing a priestly nation, Ezekiel presented a blueprint for their return to the Promised Land. The priests and Levites were to have jurisdiction in all religious matters and the civil leader was to provide support by enforcing the laws. Because of his detailed schema, he is considered by many to be the father of post-exilic Judaism.[27]

Reflection:

1. How have our religious beliefs inhibited God's action in our lives?

2. If we are God's chosen nation, how have we upheld His/Her reputation to the peoples of the world?

FORMATION OF THE PENTATEUCH

"By the rivers of Babylon we sat mourning and weeping when we remembered Zion… If I forget you, Jerusalem, may my right hand wither. May my tongue stick to my palate" (Ps. 137:1, 5). The Psalm captures the grief and yearning of the people in exile (597-538 B.C.E.).

The Babylonians allowed their captives to establish businesses and create a new life for themselves. As the years passed, some of the descendants of the original exiles began to look upon their surroundings as home. They settled down and maintained a Jewish community for twenty-five hundred years.

For others, the exile was a time to reflect on their religious heritage. The Deuteronomic authors completed their theological commentary on the monarchy. Others began compiling the oracles of the prophets. The priestly leaders composed the final edition of the Pentateuch: Genesis, Exodus, Numbers, Leviticus and Deuteronomy. These books are the Torah, since they express the foundational "Teachings" of their identity. The Pentateuch exemplifies a complex process involving the compilation of many different sources.

If I were invited to write a history of my family, I would begin by asking my maternal and paternal grandparents what they knew and remembered about their past. I would record the memories they shared about life in the old country: the customs, traditions, occupations and celebrations. I would ask about their journey to America. What motivated them to leave everything behind and venture forth to a strange land? I would collect any written materials such as letters, diaries or journals that would help me to understand who they were and how they lived. Once I gathered as much information as was available, I would organize it in a narrative. After completing a rough draft, I would have someone edit it for grammar and content before having the family review the research. Considering the project to be invaluable, they would have it professionally written and bound in a leather cover.

The Torah was compiled in much the same manner. The priestly authors wrote the Jewish family history using oral, written and liturgical sources hundreds of years old.

The vast majority of Scripture scholars accept the basic documentary theory that posits the four major sources of the Pentateuch as J (a German acronym for Yawist), E (Eloist), D (Deuteronomist) and P (Priestly). Each tradition reveals a different perspective and understanding of God.

The J source, written around 950 BCE during the reign of Solomon, shows how Yahweh's plan for the Hebrews began with creation and culminated with the settlement of the Promised Land. The E tradition, written around 850, reflects the concerns of the northern kingdom after the division of Israel. Unlike the J source that pictured Yahweh in human form, E pictures God as more transcendent. The author uses Elohim, the more generic term for God, who communicates through clouds, angels and dreams. Much of the E tradition has been lost, but what we do have was combined with J to form the JE epic after the fall of the northern kingdom in 722. The D tradition represents a school of writers who not only wrote the Book of Deuteronomy, but the history of Israel that included Joshua, Judges, 1&2 Samuel and 1& 2 Kings. The Deuteronomic theology teaches that fidelity to God's covenant means success, and infidelity leads to failure. The Priestly tradition, written around 550, emphasizes Israel's vocation as a priestly people set apart for worship. It focuses on laws governing liturgy, feast days, sacrifice, tithing and anything that would enhance their call to holiness. Scholars believe that members of the Priestly school combined all four traditions to form the Pentateuch between 550 and 500. Several texts in the final edition are confusing because the sources are interwoven (see appendix 1).

The exiles understood that their laws, customs and rituals were not museum pieces to be preserved for posterity, but a living tradition God used to address their current situation. This is why the author known as Second Isaiah (40-55) envisions Cyrus, the king of Persia, as the new Moses, sent by God to free the people from the Babylonian Pharaoh.

What do these sacred books have to tell us today?

1. God is the creator of the universe and made us in the divine image and likeness.

2. We were meant to live in harmony with God, one another and all of creation.

3. Adam and Eve, Cain and Abel, the stories of Noah and the Tower of Babel reflect our rebellious nature because we want to be Lord of our own lives.

4. Sin destroys the harmony intended by our Creator and sets us against one another and creation.

5. God does not abandon us, but lovingly reaches out to free us from the Pharaohs that control our lives. The Divine Liberator continues to hear the cries of those oppressed by personal addictions, those enslaved by destructive relationships, oppressive work environments and social policies that undermine human dignity.

6. The 613 Torah laws are meant to restore and maintain the harmony destroyed by sin. They remind us that all of life is sacred: the exalted and mundane, marriage and money, liturgy and latrines because our God is the God of life.

Reflection:

1. What does the Documentary hypothesis say about the formation of Scripture and fundamentalism?

2. What does it say about the Bible as a Living Word?

CREATION: Gen: 1:1-2:4

The story of creation, reflecting ancient traditions, is a masterpiece of literature and revelation composed by the priestly (P) source during the Babylonian exile around 550 BCE. The once glorious nation of Israel, under the kingship of David and Solomon, was totally defeated, and, separated from their homeland, the people were living in captivity. Observing the prosperity of their pagan captors, they questioned their identity as God's chosen community and nearly abandoned their faith. Writing as a theologian and not a scientist, the priestly author's purpose was to emphasize God's greatness and reaffirm to the Israelites their dignity as a covenanted people.

The cosmology of the text reflects the understanding of the universe common to the Middle East at that time. The firmament was like a giant dome over the earth protecting it from the waters above. Hanging from the dome were the sun, moon and stars. The dome also contained floodgates that God would open to allow the waters above to fall in the form of rain. The earth was like a huge saucer resting on stabilizing pillars. The waters beneath appeared above ground as oceans, lakes and rivers.

The structure of the poem is such that the 1st, 2nd and 3rd days represent the infrastructure that corresponds to the 4th, 5th and 6th days. God created the day and night on the 1st day and the sun, moon and stars on the 4th day.[28] It is important to note that the author simply refers to the sun and moon as the greater and lesser lights, a deliberate attempt to undermine the divinity attached to them by the Babylonians.

The formation of the sky and water corresponds to the creation of birds and fish. The land and vegetation provided the environment for animals and humans.

The text directly undermines many of the creation myths that existed in the Middle East at the time. Marduk, the Babylonian god, created the heavens and earth by killing Tiamat, the mother of all the living, and splitting her body in half.[29] Instead of the chaos and violence that typified such stories, the priestly author portrays God as creating by means of a simple command: "let there be light" and there was light.

The narrative is structured to emphasize God as resting on the seventh day. Our dignity as people is the celebration of holy leisure with our Creator freeing us from the mistaken notion that we are indispensable, enslaving us to our work. The Sabbath rest expresses our trust in the Creator, and affords us the opportunity to take time to interact with one another and appreciate the beauty that surrounds us. [30]

The author reminds us of our vocation as co-creators with God bringing creation to fulfillment through just stewardship. Because the Creator needs living icons to accomplish the Divine plan, God created men and women equal in the Divine image. Such an idea was extremely radical in the patriarchal societies of the Middle East and continues to challenge many cultural beliefs today.

The narrative also states that sexuality and children are a blessing. Unfortunately, much of our religious history has distorted the beauty of sexual expression, resulting in a backlash of sexual promiscuity. Despite all the misuse, sex is a form of Divine energy that connects us to another. When we experience that connection in the core of our being, we are standing on sacred ground because the basis of life is relational (Trinitarian).

One of the most interesting things about the narrative is the author's belief that humans and animals should ideally be vegetarians, reflecting the vision of Isaiah where the wolf is the guest of the lamb (Is. 11:6-9). People and animals should not have to destroy life for food. The Creator has provided green plants for our nourishment.

The story of creation continues to inspire and challenge us to live in harmony. We are reminded that the universe is good, and we need to live in reverence and awe of what God has given us. Each person is created in the image of the Creator, and deserves to be treated with respect and dignity. This is the fundamental principle underlying our value for life and our vocation to create a just society.

Reflection:

1. What is your reaction to this narrative being used to deny scientific evidence of evolution?

2. What does this text say about our environment?

ADAM AND EVE: Gen: 2:4-3:2

Reading this text leads one into a totally different literary atmosphere than the first creation story. The highly structured formula of chapter one gives way to a picturesque narrative where a variety of scenes are blended together to produce a marvelous story of charm and simplicity. Unlike the priestly (P) account in the story of creation that portrays God as transcendent, the Yawist (J) tradition portrays God as humanlike. Yahweh is a potter molding the clay of the earth, a gardener planting trees, a companion walking in the garden, and a seamstress sewing clothes for the disobedient couple. This story dates back to 950 BCE near the end of Solomon's reign. The author was struggling with the issue of human rebellion in light of God's total graciousness.

The story of Adam and Eve can be broken down into four scenes. [31] Reflecting the priestly tradition of God sharing Divine life with us humans, scene I (Gn.2:4-17) begins with God molding Adam from the dust of the ground (Adamah in Hebrew) and breathing the spirit (ruah) of life into him.

God then plants a garden and places the man in it. Eden (pleasure in Hebrew) symbolizes the Creator's total generosity in providing for the first humans. Adam's vocation was to till and care for the garden. He was permitted to enjoy everything in paradise except the fruit of the tree of good and evil (a Hebrew way of saying total knowledge).

Each of us is given gifts and talents to create a better world. We are blessed with unbelievable freedom to accomplish our task, but our liberty is tempered by our responsibility to the larger community. We fulfill our destiny when we maintain the balance between our vocation, freedom and obligation.[32]

In scene II (2:17-25) the Lord provides a suitable helpmate for Adam. The creation of woman demonstrates that she is equal to man in every manner and is called to work with him in maintaining the garden. When Adam looks upon the woman, he does not name her as he does the other creatures. Naming another is a sign of power over them. He simply rejoices. "This at last is flesh of my flesh and bone of my bones." The author reminds us that we are not meant to live alone. We find our fulfillment living in harmony with God, one another and all of creation. The end of the scene expresses the union of the man and woman: they were "naked and not ashamed."

In scene III, the wonderful order established by the Creator becomes unraveled. The serpent encounters the woman and challenges her to analyze God's prohibition about eating the forbidden fruit. He distorts the prohibition by stating that God forbade eating fruit from any tree in the garden. The woman quickly clarifies the command, but makes it more stringent, saying she was not even allowed to touch the tree of knowledge. Implying she would become self-sufficient, "you will be like God," the serpent enticed the woman to eat the forbidden fruit, thus destroying the harmony intended by the Creator.[33]

In the context of the story the serpent is simply a tool used to advance the plot, but the serpentine tactic also reflects how we avoid God by talking about God. Discussion is always safer than encounter, because it moves us from the relational to the conceptual. Identification of Satan with the snake was a much later development in Christian theology.[34]

Scene IV is the trial and judgment. Instead of becoming like God, the couple, attempting to conceal their shame, cowers in fear. Anxiously searching for the disobedient duo, the Gardener eventually finds them hiding in the bushes. When challenged, the man responds by blaming his wife, who in turn blames the serpent. Adam not only blames Eve, but also names her, demonstrating his superiority and reflecting the subordinate role of women in patriarchal societies to this day. The narrative ends with Adam and Eve being driven from the garden.

The text reminds us that we all have eaten of the tree of knowledge sometime during our formative years. We reached a point in our development when we acquired a dualistic consciousness, no longer viewing life as safe, unified and interrelated, but fearful, separate and fragmented. Just as Adam and Eve felt alienated from each other and God after eating the forbidden fruit, we, feeling the shame of our nakedness, have entered a state of alienation, expressed as inadequacy, insecurity and unworthiness. Like Adam and Eve, we lost our original sense of self as children of God, and developed a false identity based on superficial accomplishments and internalized messages. God sees us in our nakedness and clothes us in love. This experience frees us from the shame that enslaves us and restores us to our original dignity. This love is often expressed through another human who knows us completely and remains faithful through the good times and bad. These grace-filled relationships can gradually lead us to a mature conscious-ness, allowing us to experience the union of all creation once again.

Reflections:

1. In what ways do we continue to eat of the Tree of Knowl-edge?

2. Does God fear such knowledge preferring ignorance to autonomy?

CAIN AND ABEL (Gen: 4:1-16)

The Yawist (J) wrote this narrative as a theologian and not a histo-rian. Understanding his intention prevents us from asking irrelevant questions: where did the other people come from if Cain and Abel were Adam and Eve's first children?

Once humans began living outside of the garden, the symbol of unity, their behavior reflects a destructive pattern of fear, jealousy, envy, hatred and violence. Throughout the Bible, brothers and sisters con-tinually judge and condemn one another by rejecting the Divine mandate to live in this world on God's terms.

This narrative starts with the birth of Cain and Eve's exclamation: "I have produced a man with the help of the Lord!" (Gn. 4:1) All of life is a gift from God, and it is a mother's privilege to share in this cre-ative act. Abel means "puff" or "breath"—rather appropriate for one whose life was cut short.

The story reports that Cain was a farmer and Abel was a shepherd. The trouble began when the two brothers came forward to present the fruits of their labors to the Lord.

For whatever reason, God chose Abel's offering over Cain's. There is nothing in the story to indicate that Cain acted in an evil manner (1 Jn. 3: 12) or that he lacked faith as suggested in Hebrews(11:4).

It is also important to note that the author was writing in a culture that favored the firstborn son with special privileges. Yet, throughout the book of Genesis, the firstborn does not fare well. God chose Abel, Isaac and Jacob over their older brothers: Cain, Ishmael and Esau. The Yawist (J) makes it clear that life is often unfair, and God is free to act in whatever manner God chooses.

Seeing how angry Cain became over his rejection, Yahweh challenged him to do what was good or be overpowered by the force of sin within him. Contrary to some theological opinions, Cain was not the victim of original sin; he was still able to choose the right path. Unfortunately, he did not control the power of his anger, unleashing his fury on his brother Abel.

When God questioned Cain about Abel, he disavowed any responsibility. "Am I my brother's keeper"(Gn.4:9)? Once convicted of murder and sentenced to be a wanderer, removed from the presence of God, his arrogance turned to anguish. Although Cain was punished for his crime, Yahweh responded to him with grace, placing the mark of protection on his forehead. [35]

The story reminds us that each of us are challenged daily to respond to our brothers and sisters in a manner that preserves our intended unity. We are confronted with a God who is free to bestow his blessings in a manner that is arbitrary and seemingly unfair. Envy, jealousy and anger are forces lurking within us as we compare our life's situation with those around us. The passions that drove Cain to murder are no different than the judgments we make daily about each other. Why isn't life fair? Why does God seem to bless some people more than others? The Lord does not answer our questions. He/She simply repeats the warning to Cain: "Sin is a power lurking within you, but you can control it."

Reflection:

1. What does "being our brother's keeper" mean to you?

2. How do you deal with your feelings of envy or jealousy?

Noah and the Ark (Gen: 6:5-8:12)

The story of Noah and the Ark captures the imagination of children and adults alike. It combines the Yawist (J) and Priestly (P) traditions in such a manner that the narrative flows smoothly despite the repetitions and inconsistencies. A detailed reading of the story will show that 6:5 (J) and 6:11-12 (P) is just one set of doublets contained in the narrative. In the priestly version, Noah is instructed to bring two of every animal into the ark, while the Yawist version has God telling Noah to take seven pairs of clean animals and one pair that are unclean. The clean animals would be used for sacrifice; the unclean for propagation.

Legends of a primeval flood existed among ancient peoples throughout the world. Differing greatly in detail, they all seemed to testify to some catastrophic disaster in antiquity. The Gilgamesh epic (appendix II) written in Babylon around 2000 (BCE) was the primary source for the Noah narrative. The authors were inspired to rework the ancient myth and adapt it to Israel's faith. However, they had a dilemma: how could a merciful God cause a universal disaster, and would God do it again?

The story begins with God's judgment upon humanity for rebuffing its God-given identity. Creation and Creator were denied their real character. The story reveals the pain in the heart of Yahweh struggling with the rejection. It is not the story of an angry tyrant, but the pathos of a troubled parent grieving over the alienation. Humankind's evil heart troubles God's loving spirit.[36]

The narrative reminds us that God is free to take away the gifts given us and is at liberty to begin a new creation. Throughout history, the Giver has been identified with the gift, and fallaciously presumed to preserve what was given. This myth was exposed during the Assyrian and Babylonian invasion and destruction of the northern and southern kingdoms respectively. How could this possibly happen? They were God's chosen people. This same narrative has repeated itself with the decline of the Roman, Spanish, French and British empires, each one believing they were divinely chosen.

The story tells us that the Creator not only destroyed the world, but brought about a new creation symbolized by Noah and his family. Unlike the rest of the human family, Noah is totally obedient, accepting his identity and allowing God to be God as reflected in the refrain: "Noah did just as the Lord had commanded him" (Gn.7:5).

After the destruction, the Lord entered into a new covenant with *all of creation*, symbolized by the rainbow, a pledge of Divine faithfulness providing security and stability to the world. The agreement reaffirmed humanity's sovereign position within creation and allowed the killing of animals for food, ending the paradisiacal harmony by permitting the use of violence. The flood did not change the human condition, as we continue to rebel against our Creator. It transformed God. The text reminds us that God acts on our behalf despite our rebellious hearts, because unconditional love is inherently divine. At issue is God's integrity. "I will prove the holiness of my great name" (Ez. 36:23).[37]

God ordered Noah to bring two of every kind of creature on board: male and female, the clean and unclean, the violent and the tame, locking them inside—a metaphor for our lives. The Lord has locked us all together on this planet: Caucasian, Hispanic, African, Asian and Native American, with our multiplicity of beliefs as Christians, Jews, Muslims, Hindus, Buddhists, Shintos, agnostics and atheists, forcing us to live with the differences and polarities that separate us from one another. We have to learn to cope with the inconsistencies, tensions and weaknesses of our common humanity by our willingness to see life through the eyes of another.

Reflection:

1. Why does God continue to allow natural disasters that kill thousands (i.e. Tsunamis)?

2. How does the imagery of the ark connect with our global reality?

TOWER OF BABEL (GEN. 11: 1-9)

Our final pre-historical narrative, written by the Yahwist (J), concerns the use and purpose of verbal communication, suggesting that our multiple languages reflect humanity's rebellion and disobedience. Echoing the harmony that existed in Eden, everyone spoke the same tongue.

Congregating in Shinar, an ancient name for Babylon, the people decided to build a city with a tower reaching to the heavens, refusing God's command: "be fruitful and multiply, fill the earth and subdue it" (Gn. 1:28). The people wanted to maintain their common language and create a unified living environment, independent of God.

With a hint of satire, the author tells us that God "came down" to view the project and to intervene in their grandiose plan. Punishing their disobedience while fulfilling the original mandate, God scattered the people throughout the earth, resulting in numerous tongues and cultures. Despite the diversity, unity could be maintained by allowing God to be God, one who desires our cooperation as co-creators and works to bring creation to fulfillment.

Throughout history Pharaohs, Caesars, Kings, Popes, Presidents and CEOs of multi-national corporations have abused their power in vain attempts to fashion a world according to their own designs. Any effort that ignores our divinely established identity is doomed to fail.

The text also reminds us that language is critical for the shape and quality of human community. It determines how we relate to each other; how we conduct business and arrange power. Conservative language expresses our need for security and the status quo. It is ideological jargon used by civil and religious leaders to preserve their power and control the masses. Music, poetry, philosophy and art give expression to new possibilities evoking an alternative form of consciousness. These linguistic tools allow prophets to give voice to God's foolishness in challenging the conventional wisdom.[38]

This text is often counterbalanced with Acts 2. Unlike the story of Babel where people lost their ability to communicate with each other, the Pentecost text tells us that everyone understood the language inspired by the Holy Spirit. God's language is universal and speaks to the human heart. Unfortunately, there is much that passes for "God talk" that is simply a reflection of the type of Babel manifested in this story. Spirit language is not judgmental, self-righteous, elitist, violent, fearful or condemnatory. The language of God is loving, compassionate, forgiving, freeing, healing, non-violent and challenging. It speaks to our deepest yearnings, and is spoken only by those in union with the heart of God. Pentecost reminds us of our original calling; we are to go to all parts of the world revealing the heart of the Creator.

Reflection:

1. What are our towers of Babel?

2. What would you describe as authentic God-talk and why?

POST-EXILIC PERIOD

The books of the Old Testament are divided into three categories. The Torah, or teaching, includes Genesis, Exodus, Numbers, Leviticus and Deuteronomy. The Prophets not only contain the prophetic literature, but the Deuteronomic history expressed in Joshua, Judges, 1&2 Samuel and 1&2 Kings. The final collection of documents, called the Writings, reveals a wide variety of genres and concerns reflective of the ever changing socio-political realities from the exile 597 (BCE) to about 100 (BCE).

"The hands of compassionate women boiled their own children to serve them as mourners' food in the downfall of the daughter of my people" (Lam. 4:10). An eyewitness to this horror was the author of Lamentations. In the wake of Jerusalem's destruction (587), his five poems gave voice to the profound grief and unquenchable hope of a devastated people.

"Comfort, give comfort to my people, says your God. Speak tenderly to Jerusalem, and proclaim to her that her service is at an end and her guilt expiated" (Is. 40 1-2). Reading the signs of the times, an unknown prophet labeled second Isaiah, recognized the Persian leader Cyrus as the messiah, the Divine Liberator anointed to set the exiles free (Is. 44:28). Cyrus viewed himself as a patron of the gods. Following his victory over the Babylonian empire, he encouraged his various subjects to return to their roots and religious traditions. His edict of liberation (538 BCE) not only freed the Jews, but provided the financial support for the rebuilding of the temple.

Those who chose to return home discovered the process of resettling the land and rebuilding much more onerous than the idealized vision of the prophet. How could the exilic community integrate with those who remained behind? How could they reclaim their family heritage now possessed by new owners? How should they deal with their Samaritan neighbors who offered to help rebuild the temple? How should they define themselves without the political identity of the monarchy? The chronicler recorded this period in 1&2 Chronicles, Ezra and Nehemiah, reinterpreting history from the time of David to show Israel's vocation as a worshipping community not a political entity.

Nehemiah and Ezra impacted the post-exilic community by imposing strict criteria for membership based on genealogy and fidelity to the Torah. They prohibited intermarriage and forced the breakup of marriages already contracted. They rebuffed the Samaritans' offer to rebuild the temple, creating an ongoing animosity lasting into the Christian era. Intending to preserve their Jewish identity amidst cultural pressures corroding their core values, their reforms also created a false sense of elitism and a rigid legalism.

Two books challenged this sense of privilege. Ruth is the story of a Moabite woman who became King David's great grandmother. Jonah is a satirical portrayal of a reluctant prophet pouting because God showed compassion for the evil Ninevites, who repented after hearing Jonah's message.

The book of Esther demonstrated the courage required to live faithfully as a Jew in a gentile culture. The heroic exploits of Queen Esther and her cousin Mordecai saved their people from the genocidal plot of the evil Haman giving rise to the feast of Purim. This annual celebration permits the drinking of enough wine that the distinction between "Blessed be Mordecai" and "Cursed be Haman" becomes blurred.

The Persian Empire came to an end at the hands of Alexander the Great, who conquered the known world by the age of thirty. Alexander believed his divine mission was to unite his empire under the auspices of Greek culture. He died in 323 (BCE) before his 33rd birthday. The process of Hellenization was left to his four generals, who divided his kingdom. The Ptolemies, centered in Alexandria, controlled Palestine, while the more aggressive Seleucids dominated

Syria from their capitol in Antioch. Under the leadership of Antiochus III, the Seleucids eventually captured the Palestinian territory. His successor, Antiochus IV, who gave himself the humble surname Epiphanes (God manifest), attempted to force Hellenism on his Jewish subjects. In 165 (BCE), he set up an altar to Zeus in the temple and demanded ritual sacrifice using swine. This "abomination of desolation" was the final straw along with the prohibition of circumcision and the destruction of sacred scrolls.

Mattathias, a village priest, refused to comply with the royal orders and initiated a revolt that precipitated a guerrilla war headed by his son Judas, nicknamed the "hammer" or Maccabeus because of his hard-hitting tactics. In 165, Judas won a decisive victory and negotiated peace. The Temple was rededicated, inaugurating Hanukah (Feast of Lights) celebrated annually on the 25th of the Hebrew month of Keslev (sometime between late November and late December). The history of these events are recorded in the books of Maccabees.

It was during this period of Hellenization in rural Palestine that a new movement began to emerge fueled by religious conservatism and nationalistic desire for independence. This group of "pious ones"or Hasidim were the forerunners of the Pharisees.

Amidst the horrors of persecution experienced under Antiochus IV, an unknown Hasidic author composed the Book of Daniel expressing the belief that God is in control of history and the people must remain faithful at all costs. The first six chapters depict the Hasidic hero Daniel remaining obedient to the Torah despite a fiery furnace or lion's den. Written in an apocalyptic style, chapters 7-12 show the war with Antiochus as part of a much larger drama involving God's battle with the forces of evil. The bizarre imagery and symbols were a religious Morse code, understood by people of faith, but gibberish to their enemies. Another feature of Apocalypticism is to project a current crisis back to an earlier time of persecution. Thus the Book of Daniel situates the persecution under Antiochus during the Babylonian reign of Nebuchadnezzar.

Having been raised in an atmosphere of sexual repression, it is a testimony to God's creative generosity that the Song of Songs is included among our sacred texts. The highly erotic poems express the divine plan for the fully integrated person. Devoid of any overt religious content, the text expresses the belief that human intimacy is a reflection of divine love.

The Book of Psalms reveals a long history of developments dating back to King David. These prayers give expression to our varied communal and private experiences of God.

The remaining manuscripts listed among the Writings are the Wisdom books: Proverbs, Ecclesiastes and Job. Catholics and Orthodox also include Ecclesiasticus and Wisdom.

Reflective Questions:

1. How does one maintain faith and hope in a loving God amidst such evils as the Holocaust, ethnic cleansing, human trafficking, forced conversions and natural disasters?

2. "To love another is to see the face of God!" Why or why not?

DEUTERO- ISAIAH

One of the most influential writings on the New Testament is a section of Isaiah (40-55) known as Deutero or Second Isaiah. His message of comfort and hope continues to influence those who long for a new beginning, feel overwhelmed by the idols of capitalism, question the meaning of suffering or doubt the power of God's word.

The exile created an existential crisis for the Israelites. Feeling abandoned and doubting Yahweh's ability to compete with the Babylonian deities, the people were losing hope of ever returning home. Amid this calamity, an unknown prophet stepped forward proclaiming a new exodus. "Can a mother forget her infant, be without tenderness for the child of her womb? Even should she forget, I will never forget you" (Is. 49:15). Reading the signs of the times, the prophet recognized the Persian king Cyrus as the new Moses, chosen as God's liberator.

The exodus from Babylon was not just a repeat of the journey from Egypt. "Remember not the events of the past... See, I am doing something new! Now it springs forth; do you not perceive it" (43:18-19)? Unlike the previous journey, the exiles will travel on a super highway with every valley filled and mountain leveled (40:4). God will guide them like a shepherd (40:11) providing food and water (49:10), opening a new passage through the sea (51:10) and reconquering the Promised Land (49:8-12).

Mark's Gospel begins with the prophet, John, reinterpreting this message of liberation: "Prepare the way of the Lord, make straight his paths" (Mk. 1:3). Just as Second Isaiah proclaimed Cyrus as the new Moses, the Baptist declares Jesus as God's anointed to lead us into a new way of living.

Reminding us that our God is a redeemer and not a punisher—a lesson often neglected in our religious tradition, the magnificent poetry of the prophet also addresses our personal and communal experiences of exile: "Fear not, for I have redeemed you; I have called you by name; you are mine" (43:1). Today, the voices of liberation are heard through Richard Rohr, Walter Brueggemann, Elizabeth Johnson, Jorge Bergoglio, Kailash Satyarthi and many other visionaries.

No Old Testament Book emphasizes monotheism like Second Isaiah. Assessing the religious underpinnings of the Babylonian domination system, he critiqued their deities as human creations (Is. 46:1-7). Although the first commandment of the Decalogue demands loyalty to Yahweh, the history of the people reveals a belief in other lesser gods. When the Israelites entered the Promised Land they accepted Yahweh as their Redeemer, but they turned to the fertility gods for farming. Second Isaiah clarified God's role as redeemer and creator: "Thus says the Lord, your redeemer, who formed you from the womb, I am the Lord who made all things... I am the Lord, there is no other, there is no God besides me..." (Is. 44:24, 45:5).

Just as the Babylonians created gods in their own image to justify their socio-economic and political systems, we continue to do the same. Our deities are not made of gold, silver or wood, but power, profit and possessions supported by civil religion under the rubric of patriotism.

The exile forced the people to reflect on their vocation as God's chosen. Second Isaiah wrote four Servant Songs (42:1-4, 49:1-6, 50:4-9, 52:13-53:12) redefining their calling as service to the nations. Contrary to its privileged status, taught by Ezra and Nehemiah, Israel was called to suffer as expressed in the fourth song: "He was spurned and avoided by men, a man of suffering… Like a lamb led to slaughter… he was silent and opened not his mouth…. Through his suffering, my servant shall justify many…Because he surrendered himself to death, he shall take away the sins of many" (53:3,7,11-12). Israel's suffering revealed God's pathos for all people, mending broken relations and reconciling the world. When asked by the Ethiopian eunuch about the meaning of this passage, Philip reinterpreted this text as the theological underpinnings of Jesus' life (Acts 8:32-35).

Finally, the prophet addresses the authority of God's word. Influenced by the priestly creation story (Gn. 1:1-2:4) which demonstrates the power of the Divine word in bringing about creation, Second Isaiah reiterates the theme: "Though the grass withers and the flower wilts, the word of our God stands forever" (40:8). "For just as from the heavens the rain and snow come down and do not return there till they have watered the earth…. So shall my word be that goes forth from my mouth; it shall not return to me void, but shall do my will, achieving the end for which I sent it" (55:10-11). Following the teaching of Second Isaiah, the author of Hebrews says: "Indeed, the word of God is living and effective, sharper than a two-edged sword, penetrating even between the soul and spirit… able to discern reflections and thoughts of the heart" (Hb. 4:12). The power of the word is also expressed in the Second Letter to Timothy: "You cannot imprison the word of the Lord"[39] (2Tm. 2:9).

Ironically, many Scripture loving people have imprisoned God's word in the chains of fundamentalism. Trapped in the belief that the Bible is God's inerrant word devoid of human influence, they insist the texts must be interpreted literally and understood factually. This narrow paradigm, limiting any imaginative reinterpretation, identifies truth with fact. In order to unchain the power of the word, we must open ourselves to a metaphorical paradigm which allows us to explore all the possibilities of a given text and frees us to creatively reinterpret it in differing historical circumstances. Second Isaiah not only brought comfort to a people in exile, his message inspired a number of New Testament writers and, 2500 years later, continues to inspire.

Reflection:

1. Who are the people that offer you a message of hope and comfort and why?

2. How has the Word of God impacted your life?

PSALMS

The Book of Psalms, Psalter or Tehillim (Hebrew for praises) give expression to Israel's faith from the time of David to the post- exilic period. The psalter reflects a long editorial process which gathered numerous poems and songs from differing contexts into the present arrangement. There does not appear to be a thematic outline, but it is evident the psalter is composed of several collections of hymns accompanied by music composed primarily for communal worship.

Reminiscent of the Torah, the psalter is divided into five section: Ps. 1-41, a collection of hymns from the early southern kingdom; 42-72, northern kingdom psalms; 73-89, temple singers' songs; 90-106, royal psalms honoring Yahweh or the king; and 107-150, a second set of royal praises. Each section concludes with a doxology culminating with psalm 150: "Let everything that has breath give praise to the Lord" (150:6)![40]

The Psalms, voicing communal and individual feelings, range from praise and thanksgiving to lament. The first psalm, expressive of the wisdom tradition, praises the study of the Torah: "Happy those who do not follow the counsel of the wicked, nor go the way of sinners, nor sit in the company of scoffers. Rather the law of the Lord is their joy: God's law they study day and night" (Ps. 1:1-2).

A number of psalms express the anger and pathos of those searching for answers to injustice and suffering. "Why God, have you cast us off forever" (Ps. 74:1)? "My God, My God, why have you abandoned me" (Ps. 22:2)? "How long, Lord, will you utterly forget me" (Ps. 13:2)? Hear, Lord, my plea for justice; pay heed to my cry" (Ps. 17:1).

St. Augustine's dictum: "my heart is restless until it rests in thee, my Lord,"[41] is reflected in Psalm 63: "O God, you are my God—for you I long! For you my body yearns; for you my soul thirsts, Like a land parched, lifeless and without water" (63:2).

Psalm 118 expresses gratitude over God's enduring love. "Give thanks to the Lord, who is good, whose love endures forever. Let the house of Israel say: God's love endures forever… Let those who fear the Lord say, God's love endures forever" (1-4).

Exodus 23:17 required all men to journey to Jerusalem for the three major feasts of Passover, Pentecost and Tabernacles. Psalms 120-134 was a hymnbook used by pilgrims as they climbed Mt. Zion on their way to the temple. "I rejoiced when they said to me, 'let us go up to the house of the Lord.' And now our feet are standing within your gates, Jerusalem" (122:1-2). "When the Lord restored the fortunes of Zion, then we thought we were dreaming… The Lord has done great things for us" (Ps. 126:1-3).[42]

Although the psalms were communal in nature, they nourished individual piety. A number of psalms gave voice to the suffering of personal illness. "Lord… incline your ear to my cry… Because of you my friends shun me; you make me loathsome to them… My only friend is darkness" (88:2, 3, 9, 19).

Admitting sinfulness and begging for forgiveness, Psalm 51 typifies the penitential psalm. "Have mercy on me, God, in your goodness; in your abundant compassion blot out my offense. Wash away all my guilt, from my sin cleanse me… A clean heart create for me, God; renew in me a steadfast spirit" (3-4,12).

Psalm 139 powerfully expresses God's intimate knowledge of each person. "Lord, you have probed me and know me: you know when I sit and when I stand; you understand my thoughts from afar… Even before a word is on my tongue, Lord, you know it all…. You formed my inmost being; you knit me in my mother's womb. I praise you, so wonderfully you made me; wonderful are your works" (2-4,13).

The psalms demonstrate the powerful faith of the Jewish people throughout the vicissitudes of life. They trusted their relationship with God enough to voice their complaints, challenging injustice and questioning Divine wisdom, while honestly admitting their own failures, seeking forgiveness and recognizing God's mighty deeds on their behalf. They express the complexities of a living faith, not the certitudes of set doctrines. They show how liturgical actions can reveal the depth of the human spirit when not stifled by rigid regulations.

Reflection:

1. What is your favorite psalm and why?

2. What type of psalm best expresses your present circumstances: praise, lament, anger, guilt, fear or gratitude?

CARPE DIEM

"If you keep the law, the law will keep you." This sage advice along with "Don't swing the censor in the morning and Susie at night" was given to seminarians, enabling them to mature into obedient and loyal priests. The Book of Proverbs offers advice to young men to enable them to lead a successful life.

The Wisdom Tradition has a long history that dates back to the pyramids. The Wisdom scrolls, focusing on the meaning of life and how to be successful, differ greatly from the Torah and Prophets, which center on the covenant and God's mighty deeds. Egyptian philosophy influenced the practical advice on how to live the good life as expressed in Proverbs. Solomon, who married an Egyptian wife, epitomized the wise sage and was considered the author of several sections of the literature. [43]

Optimistic in outlook, the key to wisdom is "fear of the Lord" (Prv. 9:10). It is not the dread of eternal damnation, as perpetuated by the

Christian tradition, but a deep sense of reverence and awe for the unfathomed One who created our vast universe.

Challenging the optimism and teaching of the sages is the book of Ecclesiastes. Pessimistic in outlook, the book serves as a counter balance to the Wisdom scrolls. [44] "Vanity of vanities," says Quoheleth "all things are vanity" (Eccl. 1:2&12:8).

Written prior to Israel's belief in an after-life, Ecclesiastes sees death as the elephant in the room. According to Quoheleth, the Preacher, when all is said and done, you die, therefore seize the moment and live as fully as you can. There is no rhyme or reason to the seasons of our activities. "There is an appointed time for everything... A time to be born and a time to die... A time to weep and a time to laugh... A time to love and a time to hate... God has made everything appropriate for its time... without men's ever discovering from beginning to end, the work which God has done" (Eccl. 3:1-11).

God's unknowable plan is reminiscent of Job attempting to understand his suffering only to be told in essence: "I'm God, and you're human. Deal with it." Ecclesiastes is a humbling reminder that life is a mystery to be lived, not a problem to be solved. We walk in faith, not certitude. There are moments of darkness when we question the meaning of life, the existence of God and the hereafter. These "dark nights of the soul" are often necessary experiences in stripping away our arrogance and forcing us to face the utter poverty of our humanity before we can emerge with grateful hearts. No longer imprisoned by a false identity having something to prove, we become free enough to accept God's unmerited love. Paradoxically, our abject condition becomes a blessing. This is why Jesus could say: "Blessed are the destitute" (Lk. 6:20).[45] Ecclesiastes gives voice to the realization that we are partaking in a scheme beyond our imagination.

Reflection:

1. What sage advice did you receive in your formative years?

2. What dark nights of the soul have you experienced?

TRITO- ISAIAH

The book of Isaiah is divided into three parts, each reflecting differing historical circumstances. Isaiah (1-39) issues God's complaint and judgment against Jerusalem, which was destroyed 150 years later. Through Deutero-Isaiah (40-55) God remembers the destroyed city and assures its restoration. In Third Isaiah (56-66) God fulfills the Divine mandate to rebuild. [46] The author envisions a time when all nations will stream to Jerusalem to experience God's bountiful compassion (66:18). "Rejoice with Jerusalem and be glad because of her, all you who love her... Oh, that you may suck fully of the milk of her comfort, that you may nurse with delight at her abundant breasts" (66:10-11). The theme of Jerusalem running through the three sections of Isaiah as condemned, anticipated and restored, reaches its full conclusion in the Book of Revelation. "Then I saw a new heaven and a new earth... I also saw the holy city, a new Jerusalem, coming down out of heaven from God prepared as a bride adorned for her husband" (Rv. 21:1-2). This new creation is God's kingdom brought to completion. It becomes the Omega point of all reality.

Third Isaiah reflects the tension between the idealized vision of a newly created people and the reality of trying to rebuild their homeland. The images of gentiles bringing their wealth to the Jews (Is.60:5), bowing down before them (Is.60:14), tending their vineyards and flocks (Is.61:5), and the Jews being a priestly people (Is.61:6) must have seemed laughable to those just struggling to survive. Manifesting this tension, the message of Third Isaiah vacillates between comfort and condemnation.[47]

On the issue of fasting (Is.58:3), the prophet declared that true fasting involves freeing the oppressed, feeding the hungry, sheltering the homeless and clothing the naked (Is.58:6-7). Identifying with those in need, Jesus used the same criteria as the basis for the final judgment (Mt. 25).

Third Isaiah also challenges the exclusionary policies of Ezra, Nehemiah and, remarkably, the Torah by welcoming eunuchs and foreigners prohibited by Deuteronomy (23:2-4). This confrontation with the Torah reminds us that God's word is historically contextual and must be tested in differing circumstances.[48]

This radical inclusion reflects a growing understanding of God's universal embrace. The spirit of the Lord God is upon me… He has sent me to bring glad tidings to the lowly, to heal the brokenhearted, to proclaim liberty to captives and a release to prisoners" (Is.61:1-2). The prophet's mission became Jesus' self-described vocation.

Unfortunately, too many self-proclaimed followers of Jesus continue to be exclusionary in their attitudes toward those considered impure, sinful, heretical or unworthy. They live in fear of children crossing our borders, of women longing for a voice in church governance, of gays needing acceptance, of Muslims wanting peaceful co-existence and blacks advocating racial equality.

The Book of Isaiah expresses many themes reiterated and reinterpreted throughout the New Testament. These prophets impacted the spirituality of Jesus. What do they say to us?

Reflection:

1. What would Trito-Isaiah say to our present political climate concerning refugees?

2. What would he say concerning the exclusionary practices of many of our religious institutions?

SUFFERING

One of our most fundamental beliefs is that God is all-powerful and loving. This creed, however, is challenged daily by global and personal tragedies. How do we explain the staggering loss of life caused by tsunamis, hurricanes and tornadoes? How do we justify Divine goodness in the context of the AIDS epidemic in Africa, and the thousands who lose their lives monthly to malaria or other diseases caused by poor nutrition or sanitation? How can a just God allow such horrors as the Holocaust under Nazi Germany, the attempted genocide of the Tutsi's, the tragedy of 9/11, the senseless deaths of so many innocent people in Iraq and Syria? How can a compassionate

God allow a father of three to drop dead of a heart attack, a young mother to die giving birth or a child to suffer the agonies of cancer? Throughout the 1100 years that the books of the Bible were written, various answers have been proposed to such vexing questions.

In Genesis, we are told Adam and Eve's disobedience caused the pain of childbirth and the drudgery of work and death. Human sinfulness also caused the escalating evils depicted in the following chapters.

Deuteronomy tells us that obedience to God's commands will result in multiple blessings while disobedience will bring multiple curses. Jeremiah and Isaiah voiced this belief in explaining the capture of Jerusalem, the destruction of the temple and the resulting exile in Babylon.

Job challenged the simplistic understanding of suffering expressed in Deuteronomy. The story begins with God bragging to Satan, a member of the inner circle, about Job's faithfulness. Satan replies that Job needs to be tested to really determine his loyalty. With Divine permission, Satan puts Job through the worst possible day in anyone's life (Job. 1:13-20). Job passed the first test with flying colors. God then allowed Satan to afflict Job with boils from his head to his feet, leaving him seated on a dung heap. For the next 30 chapters Job's friends argued the traditional position that suffering resulted from sinfulness. Through it all, Job proclaimed his innocence. Finally Elihu comes on the scene and attempts to advance the discussion with the idea that suffering may be medicinal. Perhaps God is teaching us something through our pain. Job finally has enough and challenges God directly. God responds with an endless list of unanswerable questions, stating: "I'm Divine, you are human. There are many things you will never understand." Job humbly accepted God's response and was praised for struggling with the meaning of his pain. His friends, however, were chastised for simply mouthing beliefs that were not part of their lived experience.

The meaning of suffering took on universal significance when Antiochus IV attempted to destroy the Jewish religion and killed many innocent people in the process. The Book of Daniel began to view human anguish as part of the cosmic struggle between the forces of good and those of evil. This same belief is expressed in the Book of Revelation as John of Patmos viewed the Roman persecution of Christians as an expression of the ongoing battle between God and Satan.

Each of the above mentioned positions do shed some light on the meaning of suffering. Much of our pain is caused by our inhumanity to one another as expressed in Genesis. When we fail to surrender to God's will, our lives will always be out of sync as proposed in Deuteronomy. Suffering can be a teacher of wisdom as stated by Elihu, and there is so much of life that is beyond our comprehension as Job came to understand. The belief in a universal struggle between good and evil situates the incomprehensible agony of the Holocaust and other genocidal anguish in the context of cosmic forces.

In the person of Jesus, God does answer our questions about suffering, but in a manner that defies our wildest imagination. Affliction will always be part of the human condition, except we are no longer alone in our pain. The cross tells us that the heart of God aches with those who grieve. It reminds us that the rejected One is present with all of those deserted by Church and State. The Savior's outstretched arms will always embrace those enslaved by addictions, oppressed by fear, or trapped in the endless spiral of despair and hopelessness. The dying One never abandons those struggling with terminal illness or waiting in anguish as their child's life draws to an end. The non-violent One expresses solidarity with all victims of violence. The crucified One identifies with those who suffer needlessly.

The cross ultimately reveals that the way to life is through death. Jesus did not take away our anguish—he transformed its meaning.

Reflection:

1. How do you explain the discord between an all-powerful, loving God and human tragedy?

2. How have you experienced comfort amidst your personal suffering?

NEW TESTAMENT

U nlike the Old Testament, the twenty-seven books of the New Testament have mutual agreement between Catholics, Orthodox and Protestants. Written in Greek, the texts reflect the developing faith of various communities over a span of ninety years. Composed twenty years after Jesus' death, Paul's First letter to the Thessalonians (49-50 CE) is the earliest text. The Second letter of Peter (120 CE) is the last of the manuscripts. It was a common practice to attribute letters to venerable figures (Peter died around 64 CE). The technical term for this practice is pseudepigrapha, which includes half of the Pauline letters.

The gospels are our primary source for knowing about Jesus. The only non-Christian source is a document (90 CE) written by the Jewish historian Josephus, depicting Jesus as a wise man, a teacher and a healer, crucified by the Romans but loved by his followers known as Christians. The thirteen letters attributed to Paul and focusing on community issues, reveal very little about Jesus' life.

The earliest Christians lived with the expectation that Jesus' second coming would occur in their lifetime. In this context, the faith was transmitted orally from person to person and developed within the nascent communities. The four gospels reflect the theological understanding of their respective communities. They are not biographies, but faith documents combining the pre-Easter memory of Jesus with the post-Easter testimony adapted to their lived circumstances. As the first generation of Christians began to die, the need to collect the remembered sayings and deeds of Jesus became imperative. The Gospel of Mark (70 CE), providing the basic outline of the Master's life, became a primary source for Matthew (85 CE) and Luke (90 CE). Another source for the two gospels containing many of Jesus' teachings is a document known as "Q" (Quelle or source) written around 50 CE.

Our understanding of Jesus has been colored by the historical circumstances surrounding our creedal formulas. Fearing the divisiveness of the Arian heresy, claiming Jesus was not equal to the Father, the emperor Constantine invoked the Council of Nicea (325 CE). The council decreed Jesus was of the same substance (consubstantial) with the Father, but the heresy continued for another two centuries. The Northern barbarians were taught the Arian form of Christianity and forcibly imposed this belief on the peoples they conquered as they migrated south. Reacting to this movement, the church overemphasized Jesus' divinity to the point of undermining his humanity as defined at Chalcedon (360 CE). Reading the gospels through divinized filters distorts our attempt to understand the historical Jesus who was not experienced as the "Son of God" or "Messiah".

The disciples knew the pre-Easter Jesus as a fully human Jewish person who laughed, cried, ate, drank, slept and died. They experienced the post-Easter Jesus as a transfigured presence in their midst with divine qualities. These visions transformed a group of frightened disciples into bold evangelists. Many of the gospel texts reflect this glorified image understood as the Christ of faith.

One of the earliest creedal formulas is found in the Book of Acts. "Jesus the Nazorean was a man commended to you by God with mighty deeds, wonders and signs, which God worked through him in your midst... This man delivered up by the set plan and foreknowledge of God, you killed, using lawless men (Romans, outside of Jewish law) to crucify him. But God raised him up, releasing him from the throes of death, because it was impossible for him to be held by it" (2:22-24).

Scripture scholars have been attempting to uncover the historical Jesus buried within the gospel texts for the past two centuries. The earlier attempts revealed more the biases of the scholars than an honest profile. The tools available today are more sophisticated and enable biblical experts to develop a more objective picture. The

Roman system of peace through violence (Pax Romana), the diviniza-
tion of the emperor, an economic policy favoring the wealthy, heavy
taxation, ninety percent illiteracy, increasing numbers of displaced
and destitute people, messianic expectations, Jewish resistance and
religious practices provide the backdrop of Jesus' ministry.

Reflecting this inequality, one out of every sixteen verses in the New
Testament addresses economic issues. One out of every ten verses in
the Synoptic Gospels (Matthew,Mark,Luke) focus on the poor, high-
lighted in the Gospel of Luke with one out of seven. Jesus' proclamation of God's kingdom as a mustard seed in our midst refers to the
transformation of this world through a more just distribution of
Divine resources.

Living and teaching non-violence directly challenged the Roman system of peace through violence. His life of humble service undermined
the cultural glorification of social status. His life of self-emptying was
a counter point to Caesar's claim of divinity. His practice of meal fellowship with tax-collectors, prostitutes and those marginalized,
directly confronted the religious practices of avoiding those considered unclean or sinful. His forgiveness of sinners undercut the religious belief that God could only forgive sins through the temple priest
using the proper rituals. His healing ministry revealed the energy
available to anyone willing to act as a conduit of God's compassion.

Proclaiming the nature of God's kingdom through his words and
deeds led to his crucifixion—Jesus had turned the world of "normalcy" upside down. "God's foolishness is wiser than human wisdom, and the weakness of God is stronger than human strength" (1
Cor. 1:25). The resurrection validated His life and transformed Him
into the Cosmic Christ connecting all of reality.

Reflection:

1. The headings of Old and New Testament could imply that
   one is superior to the other. Why is this a false understanding?

2. Why has Christian formation often failed to include socio-
   economic issues as portrayed in the Gospels?

JESUS: JEWISH MYSTIC

Symbolized by his baptism, Jesus began his adult career as a disciple of John the Baptist.[49] The emerging church, embarrassed by this memory, gradually recast the incident into a post-Easter proclamation in John's gospel with the Baptist's proclaiming Jesus the Son of God (See appendix iii for the textual progression from Mark to John). Mark reports that when Jesus ascended from the water, God's Spirit descended on him. This mystical experience governed Jesus' childlike understanding of God as "abba" (daddy).

Unlike the Baptist who awaited God's imminent judgment and clean-up of this evil world, Jesus proclaimed the kingdom of God as present: transforming the Roman domination system of violence and economic inequality to a non-violent, just distribution of resources for all people. Guided by the Spirit, Jesus chose followers to participate in this transformation process.

His ministry of healing, teaching and open fellowship with those marginalized, flowed from the inner spirit received at baptism and renewed daily through prayerful solitude. "The Spirit of God is upon me… to bring glad tidings to the poor… liberty to captives… recovery of sight to the blind, to let the oppressed go free…"(Lk. 4:18-19).

Those who encountered Jesus knew they were in the presence of someone out of the ordinary. Many people were astonished at his teaching because he taught with authority not like the scribes (Mk. 1:22). His family thought he was insane and tried to take hold of him to keep themselves from further embarrassment (Mk. 3:21). The scribes thought he was possessed (Mk. 3:22). Others called him a drunk and a glutton (Mt. 11:19).

Jesus' mysticism allowed him to see everything as connected, enabling him to challenge many religious rules and rituals based on the external authority of biblical texts or the theological interpretations of various religious leaders. He was a Jew to the core of his being. He did not come to establish a new religion, but reform aspects of the tradition that oppressed those already heavily burdened. "Take my yoke upon you and learn from me, for I am meek and humble of heart; and you will find rest for yourselves, for my yoke is easy and my burden light" (Mt. 11:29-30).

Throughout history mystics have always been held suspect by the church because their authority, flowing from their subjective experience, is beyond the scope of institutional control. True mystics, not inclined to be anti-institutional, understand that the Spirit often acts outside official sanctions. [50]

This tension between external authority and subjective experience was at the heart of second and third century debates between those representing the developing institutional church and those Christians classified as Gnostics. Unfortunately, the heretical mystics developed an elitist attitude toward the larger community because they were privileged with special insight (gnosis) beyond the grasp of ordinary believers. Their "superior" knowledge created a privatized form of religion undermining the Body of Christ. A trove of gospels, epistles and other writings were discovered in 1947 near Nag Hammadi, Egypt, offering insight into their teachings. Although a few of these writings (Shepherd of Hermas or Gospel of Thomas) were considered sacred in some communities, they never received the universal approval needed for incorporation into the Bible. [51]

Fortunately, our Christian tradition has also sanctified mystics such as Teresa of Avila, John of the Cross and Julian of Norwich to validate the importance of unitive consciousness on our spiritual journey. All charisms, including mysticism, are given for building up of the community. It is not a gift given to everyone, and that is why Jesus could say to Thomas, "Blessed are those who have not seen and have believed" (Jn. 20:29).

Most of us have to walk in faith and not by the light of mystical vision. However, if we allow God's Spirit to gradually transform us, we will begin to glimpse manifestations of the kingdom developing around us. As we grow into the second half of life, our experience allows us to intellectually understand the Divine energy connecting all things. Through meditation, our reasoned understanding may sometimes lead to overwhelming flashes of unitive consciousness.

Reflection:

1. What are the strengths and weaknesses of a faith based solely on external or internal authority?

2. How do our temperament and personal experiences impact our faith vision?

JESUS PROCLAIMS THE KINGDOM

"This is the time of fulfillment. The kingdom of God is at hand. Repent, and believe the gospel" (Mk. 1:15).

Jesus' proclamation of the kingdom needs to be viewed in the context of the Roman system of power and control. When he was a toddler living in Nazareth, a rebellion broke out at the death of Herod the Great. The Roman legions destroyed the city of Sapphoris (four miles distant) and enslaved many of the men. The legions completed their suppression by capturing 2000 of the remaining rebels and crucifying them outside the city walls of Jerusalem.[52]

Herod Antipas, ruler of the Galilean province, rebuilt the city of Sapphoris and constructed Tiberius as his new capital when Jesus was in his late teens. These projects required higher taxation on a peasant population already heavily burdened. Many lost their land and became indebted to their new landowners.

Following the Assyrians, Babylonians, Persians and Greeks, Rome perpetuated the domination system benefiting the wealthy elites. After ending Rome's civil war and establishing an empire from the Atlantic to the Euphrates, from the deserts of Africa to the Danube, Caesar was decreed to be a god and honored as the "Prince of Peace." Proclaiming him "Lord" was required as a sign of allegiance.

After replacing the incompetent Herod Agrippa in 6 CE, Caesar appointed the high priest and temple authorities as collaborators in the system. As mediators of imperial rule, the Sadducees were responsible for collecting revenue for Rome while maintaining domestic order. As the center for Jewish worship, the temple was co-opted by the imperial domination system. Responses to this oppression varied from collaboration to violent and non-violent resistance.

Jesus used "kingdom of God" as a political-religious metaphor to describe what life would be like on earth if God were king instead of the lords of this world. Burning with passion for God's people, Jesus envisioned a non-violent, just distribution of resources benefitting everyone. [53]

This is why He taught the poor to pray for daily bread and the forgiveness of debts. Those displaced from their land because of high taxes or unpaid loans longed for a daily meal. When he preached his Sermon on the Plain he connected the kingdom with the wellbeing of the poor and hungry. "Blessed are you who are poor, for the kingdom of God is yours… You who are now hungry for you will be satisfied… You who are weeping for you will laugh" (Lk. 6:20-21). However, the fortunes of those who are rich, filled, laughing and well regarded will be reversed under God's rule (Lk.6:24-26).

When Jesus taught his disciples about God's kingdom, he described a radical departure from the norms of society: "If anyone wishes to be first, he shall be the last of all and the servant of all" (Mk. 9:35). You know that those who are recognized as rulers (Romans) over the Gentiles lord it over them, and their great ones make their authority felt… Whoever wishes to be great among you will be your servant; whoever wishes to be the first will be the slave of all" (Mk. 10:42).

Symbolizing equality, Jesus' meal ministry subverted the prevailing social hierarchies of his day: all were welcome to participate.

Jesus not only taught about God's passion for non-violent social justice, he lived it. When he entered Jerusalem to celebrate Passover week, he reenacted the vision of Zechariah: "See, your king shall come to you; a just savior is he, Meek and riding on an ass… He shall banish the chariot from Ephraim… The warrior's bow shall be banished, and he shall proclaim peace to the nations" (Zech. 9:9-10). He orchestrated his peaceful demonstration while Pilate and his Roman legions were trying to maintain crowd control (Mk. 11:2-3).[54]

The next day Jesus reenacted Jeremiah's prophecy (7:1-11) and symbolically destroyed the temple by driving out the money changers who made "the house of prayer for all peoples" (Is. 56:7) into a "den of thieves" (Jer.7:11). By his actions, He condemned the temple authorities for collaborating with the Roman system of injustice and violence. " The chief priests and scribes came to hear of it, and were seeking ways to put him to death" (Mk. 11:18). 55

Jesus was passionate about God's kingdom and He non-violently challenged any social, political, economic, military and religious value that supported and collaborated with Roman imperial control. Caiaphas understood the danger Jesus posed to Jewish security when he stated: "It is better for you that one man shall die instead of the people, so that the whole nation may not perish" (Jn. 11:50).

Executing Jesus was Rome's way of handling troublemakers. Crucifixion proved effective for maintaining control and security. Had the story ended there, Jesus, like so many others before him, would have disappeared from history. The Resurrection validated everything he said and did. 56Given full authority as Lord of heaven and earth (Mt. 28:18), Jesus commissions us to continue the ministry of bringing about God's kingdom.

According to the Gospel of Matthew, the final judgment is based upon our willingness to cooperate with God's plan for transforming this world. "When I was hungry... thirsty, naked, ill or in prison you responded to my needs... When did we do this Lord? Whenever you did it to the least of my brothers and sisters, you did it for me" (Mt. 25:31-46).

Being a disciple of Jesus involves more than simply accepting Him as Lord and Savior. It is a political as well as personal commitment. "Whoever wishes to come after me must deny himself, take up his cross, and follow me" (Mk. 8:34).

When we pray, "Thy kingdom come, thy will be done on earth as it is in heaven," we are expressing our willingness to let go of our kingdoms in order to non-violently transform our little worlds in accordance with Our Divine Liberator.

Reflection:

1. How did Jesus' experience of Roman Domination impact His proclamation of the Kingdom?

2. How does being a disciple of Jesus impact our political understanding?

NAZARETH: THE CHALLENGE (Lk. 4:16-30)

Its population ranging between two and four hundred residents, Nazareth was a small rural town located fifteen miles east of the Sea of Galilee and seventy miles north of Jerusalem. Sepphoris, the capitol of Galilee, destroyed by the Romans during an uprising when Jesus was a baby and rebuilt during his lifetime, was four miles south.

Most Nazarenes were farmers who either owned their own land or worked for a landlord as a sharecropper, tenant or day laborer. The fields were located outside the village where they produced olives, fruits, vegetables or animal products.[57] Politically and religiously conservative, the people were rigid and closed to outsiders; theirs was a gentile free community. Since the destruction of Sepphoris, resentment toward the Roman occupation continued to percolate.

Luke's gospel tells us Jesus entered the synagogue and read from Isaiah, chapter 61, often used to justify Israel's sense of ethnic superiority. The text envisions the golden age of the Messiah, reversing Jewish fortunes by returning control of the land and depicting the gentiles as indentured servants. Jesus concluded the reading before the section that reflected the longing of his home community (Is. 61: 4-9).

Refusing to validate their anti-gentile attitudes, he quoted a passage that expressed God's graciousness toward a Lebanese woman, a worshipper of Baal (1Kgs. 7-24), even though there were many widows in Israel who were also suffering. He also quoted the story of God curing Naaman, the Syrian general (2Kgs. 5:1-27), even though there were many lepers in Israel at the time. Coincidentally, the two gentile heroes resided in areas bordering his home region.

Reacting to Jesus' challenge to their biases, his former neighbors took him to the ridge of the town to stone him, but he walked through their midst, foreshadowing the crucifixion when he transcended death.

This story challenges our own attitudes toward those who differ from us religiously, racially, socially and sexually. God loves all her/his children, and any attempt to claim superiority simply reflects our own self-interest and spiritual immaturity.

Reflection:

1. How has your hometown impacted your family and biases?

2. How does this text relate to our attitudes toward those differing from us?

NEW WINE INTO NEW WINE SKINS

When questioned about his fasting practices, Jesus responded, "You cannot put new wine into old wineskins" (Mk. 2:22). In other words, the inauguration of God's kingdom is something so totally new it cannot be absorbed by our old consciousness. His words and deeds were attempts to expand our awareness so we could be filled with the new wine of God's unconditional love.

He taught in parables to break free of the Jewish cultural filters that inhibited the good news. When asked by a lawyer, "Who is my neighbor?" (Lk. 10:23-36), he told the wonderful story of a Samaritan hero. The Samaritans were a people despised by Jews for centuries. The parable of the prodigal son (Lk. 15) portrayed God as a Mid-eastern patriarch unlike any other. When asked by his younger son for his inheritance (the equivalent of saying, "die old man"), the father complied. When the son returned destitute seeking forgiveness, the father ran to him (patriarchs never run), embraced him and threw a party in his honor. [58]

Family honor was held in such high esteem that no one dared dishonor the family name. When Jesus' mother and siblings went to bring him home, thinking he was out of his mind (Mk. 3:21), he redefined family as anyone who listens and obeys the word of God.

Jewish law labeled certain people unclean. Tax collectors were hated because of their collaboration with the Romans. Jesus undermined the prevailing thinking by dining with Zachaeus (Lk. 19:1-10) and choosing Matthew as one of the twelve (Mk. 2:13-17). Prostitutes were easy to classify as sinners, yet Jesus praised the woman who appeared during supper and washed his feet with her tears and dried them with her hair. Simon, the leading Pharisee in the community, blinded by his religious beliefs, could not see her profound expression of love (Lk. 7:36-50).

Women were viewed as second-class citizens in a patriarchal society, yet Jesus chose Mary Magdalene to announce the resurrection to the other apostles (Jn. 20:11-18). The woman at the well became his apostle to the Samaritans despite her five husbands (Jn. 4:4-42).

Many Jews aligned themselves with the Zealots in their desire to overthrow the Romans. Jesus spoke of loving one's enemies and praying for one's persecutors. "If a soldier orders you to walk one mile, go two. If they want your shirt, give them your cloak as well." He challenged the prevailing notion that wealth, success and contentment were signs of God's blessings. "Blessed are the poor, the grieving and those who hunger and thirst for justice." The old wineskins could never contain such teachings.

Emphasizing a dualistic consciousness that divided life between the spiritual and material, heaven and earth, the divine and human, body and soul, various forms of Plato's philosophy have greatly influenced Christian theology throughout history. The material world was generally seen as imperfect if not outright evil. This divisive mindset divided us from ourselves (body vs. soul); sex was usually viewed as sinful and marriage was considered inferior to celibacy. The environment was totally at our disposal to use as we pleased, and getting to heaven was our goal with little concern for this world. This philosophy carried over into our relationships. Imitating the Jewish people of the first century, we set up our morality codes to determine who is acceptable or not. We have been reaping the destructive results of such a mindset for centuries.

Jesus' incarnation provides us with the new wineskin for a unitive consciousness. The divine and human, heaven and earth are now united. We are intertwined with our environment and can no longer rape our resources without destroying ourselves. He reminded us that sex is God's special gift that brings us into union with another. He validated our divine nature and taught us how to live as children of the same God. The divine life force flows through all people: Muslems, Hindus, Jews, Christians and atheists. Unitive consciousness respects the diversity of cultures, opinions and sexual orientations. Jesus' mission was to reconcile all things in himself. Colossians reminds us that through him everything is connected (Col. 1:15-23). This is why any spiritual leader who proclaims a message of fear and divisiveness is speaking against the unifying force of the Holy Spirit. The old wineskin of dualistic consciousness cannot contain the new wine of God's unifying and unconditional love. New wine requires new wineskins.

Reflection:

1. How has your consciousness developed as a result of your spiritual journey?

2. Who or what has had the greatest influence on your worldview?

FORGIVENESS

"Lord, if my brother sins against me, how often must I forgive him? As many as seven times?"

Jesus answered, "I say to you, not seven times, but seventy - seven times" (Mt. 18:21-22).

Forgiveness was an essential component of Jesus' healing ministry. Forgiving the sins of the paralytic, Jesus turned to the scribes who accused him of blasphemy: "Which is easier to say... Your sins are forgiven, or... Rise, pick up your mat and walk" (Mk. 2:9)? Whole-making not only involves healing the body, but mending the spirit.

When the woman was caught in the act of adultery, Mosaic Law demanded she be stoned to death (Lv. 20:10). Defying the Torah, Jesus challenged her accusers by saying, "Let the one among you who is without sin be the first to throw a stone at her"... After the crowd dispersed, he turned to the woman, saying, "Neither do I condemn you. Go, from now on do not sin anymore" (Jn. 8: 3-11).

Encountering the Samaritan woman who had five husbands and was now cohabitating, Jesus gently addressed her personal life and inspired her to become his apostle to the Samaritans. Having been insulted by his pharisaic host who neglected the basic rules of hospitality, Jesus allows a town prostitute to provide the required rituals. Addressing his host: "Her many sins have been forgiven: hence she has shown great love" (Lk. 7:47).

Passing through Jericho, Jesus spotted the vertically challenged Zacchaeus, a tax collector literally up a tree, and invited himself to supper. Touched by this grace, Zacchaeus vowed to give half his wealth to the poor and pay fourfold those he extorted. Jesus responded to him, "Today salvation has come to this house" (Lk. 19:1-10).

When asked to teach his followers how to pray, he taught them the prayer we memorized as children. A key petition is asking for forgiveness based on our own willingness to forgive (Mt. 6:9-14). In Matthew's Sermon on the Mount, Jesus reminds us that reconciliation is more important than worship. "If you bring your gift to the altar, and there recall that your brother has anything against you, leave your gift at the altar, go first and be reconciled with your brother, and then come and offer your gift" (Mt. 5:23-25).

Addressing his destitute disciples in his Sermon on the Plain, Jesus said: "Love your enemies, do good to those who hate you, bless those who curse you, pray for those who mistreat you... Be merciful as your Father is merciful... Stop judging and you will not be judged. Stop condemning and you will not be condemned... Forgive and you will be forgiven" (Lk. 6: 27-37).

The Sermon on the Plain became a lived reality in Jesus' Sermon from the Cross. When mocked and scorned, he said, "Father, forgive them; they do not know what they do" (Lk. 23:14). Also, responding to a request by one of the insurgents crucified with him, he replied, "Amen, I say to you, today you will be with me in Paradise" (Lk. 23:43).

In one of the resurrection episodes, Jesus confronts the guilt-ridden Peter. He asked his chosen leader to declare his love three times, corresponding to Peter's previous three denials. Jesus then commissions him to shepherd his sheep (Jn. 21:15-17).

Pope Francis says he wants leaders who smell like the sheep they tend. When God's forgiveness frees us daily from the stink of our own sin, we gradually develop the compassion needed to connect with those we are called to serve.

Reflection:

1. Why is forgiveness essential to Jesus' message?

2. How has forgiveness impacted your life?

THE COSMIC BATTLE (Luke 10:17-20)

This text reminds us that Christianity is not a privatized religion as Jesus sends the seventy-two disciples out in pairs. No single individual can be the Body of Christ. Even though we come from differing religious traditions, occupations and backgrounds, we have all been given the Spirit of Christ and are called to be His presence in our communities.

Excited by their success, the disciples returned from their mission anxious to share their stories. Thinking they knocked off a few demons, Jesus tells them he saw Satan fall from the sky like lightening.

In the mythology of the day, the one who controlled the sky ruled the earth. Validating their efforts, Jesus reminds them of the source of their power. "I have given you the power to tread on serpents and scorpions, and upon the full force of the enemy and nothing will harm you"(Lk.10:20). .

This text challenges us, regardless of the danger, to use the gifts and talents we have to confront evil. Jesus tells us that whenever we use our abilities to free people from the forces of death we are participating in the destruction of all evil power. Can we believe it?

Can we believe that when we teach a person to read, we are giving notice to all the forces of ignorance that their time is limited? Can we believe that whenever we hold a grieving person in our arms, we are telling all tears that they are not the final answer? Can we believe that whenever we help those who are hungry or homeless, we undermine the power of greed and the structures of poverty? Can we believe that whenever we forgive another we free them from the power of guilt and ourselves from the need for revenge? Can we believe that whenever we confront another lovingly with the truth, we are bringing freedom to those enslaved by the blindness of self-deceit? Can we believe that whenever we reach out to the outcasts of society, we are destroying the forces of prejudice, self-righteousness and narrow mindedness? Can we believe that whenever we honestly love another, we are exercising an eternal energy? Can we believe that whenever we attack evil in any way we are helping to bring about God's kingdom on earth?

Whenever we allow God's power to work through us, we are destroying the forces of evil and our names are inscribed in heaven. Can we believe it?

Reflection:

1. What cosmic struggles can you identify in your life?

2. Describe an experience where God used you to confront an evil?

POWER OF THE CROSS

The most effective way to unite a group of people is to create a common enemy. The mechanism known as scapegoating has been the basis of cultural formation since the dawn of human history. Hate works because it is efficient. Love on the other hand is chaotic, because it embraces the messiness of human existence. Love means that we are willing to accept ourselves and others with all of our warts, sins and imperfections. Hate doesn't have to bother with the evil within. We simply can project it onto someone else and focus our attention on dealing with "wickedness" out there.

However, since most of us consider ourselves good, we could never just admit our hatefulness. We have to disguise it as love in order to justify it. Under the appearance of loving one's country, we can initiate preemptive wars, torture, rape and kill innocent civilians while accusing those who oppose our efforts as unpatriotic. Under the pretext of loving one's religion, we can call for a holy war, accuse others of heresy, and condemn those who do not meet our purity codes. Under the façade of loving one's community we can vilify those who do not share our political views and ban those who are racially different. Under pretense of loving one's reputation, we can justify revenge and lack of forgiveness. Under guise of being loving parents, we can enslave our children into adulthood by manipulating them with guilt. Under the excuse of loving another, we can control, possess, abuse and deceive them while they remain passive because of their vulnerability.[59]

Our country was formed with the genocide of one race and the enslavement of another. Throughout history we have used scapegoating to control social order and accomplish the goals of those in power. Jews, blacks, homosexuals, women, liberals, conservatives and countless others have all been victimized by "justifiable" hate, and the process continues.

The turning point of human history began 2,000 years ago on a small hill outside of Jerusalem. The innocent victim was condemned by the church for blasphemy and the state for insurrection. Jesus faced the power of evil and did not succumb to revenge. He was able to embrace the wickedness and continue to love. The cross exposed the scapegoating mechanism for the lie it is. It revealed another way that was different than the usual fight or flight. [60]

"Justifiable" hate continues to work in the short term, but as our human consciousness continues to develop, the old rationalizations begin to sound empty. We are gradually beginning to realize that the dualistic thinking that perpetuates divisiveness is destructive to all people. The evil out there is simply a reflection of the evil within. When we learn to embrace our own sinfulness, we become more capable of recognizing our common humanity.

The cross unites the divine and human, heaven and earth, saints and sinners, the sacred and profane. It undermines our basic assumptions about good and evil, success and failure, strength and weakness. The cross continues to destabilize the foundations of our society by exposing the misuse of power and our false notions of love. The cross teaches the way of non-violent resistance and the value of forgiveness. Despite our continued attempts to turn the cross into a sword, it points to a culture beyond violence. In this context, the cross is the way to salvation.

Reflection:

1. How have you experienced your shadow side at work?

2. What does the cross mean for you?

PARABLES

"Jesus spoke to the crowds only in parables" (Mt. 13:34).

As a brilliant theologian and mystic, he shared his vision of reality from within the Jewish wisdom tradition using parables, stories, proverbs and lessons from nature rather than abstract concepts to teach about the kingdom of God. These literary forms capture the imagination and are understood on multiple levels. Stories and parables allow each of us to interpret them according to our life's journey. An adolescent or young adult perceives reality differently than someone who is middle age or living in the final stages of life. Unlike one-dimensional ideas appealing to our rational mind, parables engage the total person. When we grasp a concept, we feel a sense of power and control, knowing we can usually fit the new idea into our pre-conceived worldview. Stories are not meant to be grasped—they grab, pulling us into the unfolding script. When we enter into the dynamics of the parable we can experience its transforming power.

In this series, I will focus on several of Jesus' parables in their cultural settings. We will journey back to 1st century Palestine and listen to the man from Galilee and his understanding of God's vision for us.[61] He used stories to confront sensitive issues in a non-confrontational manner. Presenting opposing views in the context of story engages the audience without provoking a defensive reaction. Parables create the possibility of expanding one's consciousness to view reality with a fresh set of eyes.

After Jesus died, his sayings and stories were remembered and handed on orally in various communities. Eventually they were written down to preserve them for future generations. One text, named

"Q" (quelle or source) and composed around 50 CE, contains the teachings found in the Sermon on the Mount and a number of parables found in Matthew and Luke.

Comparing the same parable used in the two gospels demonstrates how they were modified for the individual communities. For example, in Luke's Gospel, Jesus tells the story of the Lost Sheep to challenge the righteousness of the scribes and Pharisees (15:3-6). In Matthew's Gospel (18:12-13), Jesus addresses the parable to his disciples, encouraging religious leaders to search for those who have chosen to leave the community.

Each parable has three contexts: Jesus' ministry, the gospels and our lives. Whenever possible, it is important to understand the parable as Jesus intended so we don't project our own prejudices on the text. Once we determine the original meaning, we can apply the text to our contemporary circumstances.

Jesus shocked his audience by claiming the reign of God was happening now. He was the agent inaugurating this new reality. When the Baptist, who preached a message of repentance to avoid imminent divine judgment, sent his disciples to question the validity of Jesus' ministry, they were told: "Go back and tell John what you have seen and heard: the blind regain their sight, the lame walk, lepers are cleansed, the deaf hear, the dead are raised, the poor have the good news proclaimed to them. And blessed is he who takes no offense at me" (Lk. 7:18-24).

Reflection:

1. Why are parables or stories a more effective means of communicating spiritual truths?

2. What is your favorite parable and why?

THE LOST SHEEP AND LOST COIN (Lk. 15:1-10

The Lost Sheep and the Lost Coin are twin parables addressing the issue of Pharisaic righteousness. The context for the parable of the lost sheep is the challenge to Jesus' ministry by the scribes and Pharisees.

"This fellow welcomes sinners and eats with them" (Lk. 15:2). The Holiness Code (Lv. 17-26) considered a number of people outside of the law because of moral behavior (prostitutes), physical condition (leprosy) or occupation (tax-collectors). Since eating with another was a sign of total acceptance and equality, commensality with such a person violated all religious standards.

The Holiness Code exposed the underlying politics of superiority. It guaranteed that the "saved" were divinely approved and considered morally superior to those outside of the religious system. We witness the same attitudes in many of our churches today toward Muslims, gays, illegals, the divorced and remarried, and those who had an abortion.

Jesus' ministry undercut the politics of righteousness with the politics of compassion. He challenged his accusers with three parables: the lost sheep, lost coin and lost son.

"Which of you having one hundred sheep does not leave the ninety-nine and go after the one that is lost until he finds it?" The parable describes Jesus' attackers as shepherds herding sheep. The story thus begins with a shock to his accusers' sensitivities, since shepherding was considered an "unclean" profession. The parable also indicates that it was their neglect that led to the lost sheep.[62] As religious leaders, how often have we lost parishioners because of our institutional righteousness, insensitivity, arrogance or indifference?

Finding the lost animal, the shepherd joyfully places it on his shoulders and carries it home where the community joins the celebration of the sheep's return. Expressing God's compassion, the imagery of the shepherd carrying the sheep on his shoulders became the primary Christian symbol for the first centuries.

The parable ends with the ironic statement: "There is more joy in heaven over one sinner who repents than over the ninety-nine righteous who have no need of repentance"(Lk.15:7). Jesus redefines repentance as an act of being found. The lost sheep did nothing. [63] Repentance is not a human act, but the hound of heaven constantly pursues us until we allow ourselves to be found. The parable ends with the lost sheep at home and the ninety-nine still in the wilderness.

You can't be found until you first admit that you are lost. Jesus is telling us we are all sinners, but God's compassion knows no limits.

Reflection:

1. How are the Pharisaical attitudes perpetuated in our churches?

2. Describe any experience you may have had of being found.

LOST COIN

The woman in the story represents another type of person marginalized by the culture. In the Lost Sheep, Jesus questions his accusers by saying, "What man among you would not seek after a lost sheep?" With the Lost Coin, he simply asks, "What woman who loses a coin wouldn't search for it?" It would have been the ultimate insult to say, "What woman among you...?"[64]

Worn as a necklace, the lost coin may have been part of the woman's dowry. Losing one of the ten coins was as much a symbolic loss as a monetary one. The symmetry and beauty of the necklace would have been destroyed.

Peasant women were mostly restricted to their home. They were allowed to go to the village well for water, but it was preferable for them to stay inside. In light of these cultural expectations, Jesus has the woman searching inside her home for the coin. [65] Lighting a lantern, she swept the dirt floor until she found it. Having found it, she invites her friends and neighbors to share her joy.

Like the woman in the parable, God searches until She/He finds us. The Lost Sheep and Lost Coin remind us that God never gives up.

Reflection:

1. Why do feminine images of God continue to shock our consciousness?

2. Who would you exclude from table fellowship and why?

THE LOST SON (Lk. 15:11-32)

The parable of the lost son, the third in a series Jesus used to respond to those who challenged him for eating with "sinners," begins with the youngest son asking his father for his share of the inheritance. In 1st century Palestine this was equivalent to telling one's father to "die already." A typical patriarch would have thrown his son out of the home, excommunicating him from the family and community. The older son was obligated to mediate the situation, but said nothing, indicating a rift with his brother and/or father. Ignoring conventional wisdom, the father not only granted his son's request, but allowed him to sell the land before his death, as was customary. It should be noted he also gave the older son his share of the estate.[66]

Violating the community's unwritten rules, the younger son would have antagonized a number of the villagers by trying to sell them the land. Eventually, he found a gentile buyer, further antagonizing his neighbors.[67]

Having failed his money management classes, he quickly spent his inheritance and found himself in dire straits. Desperate to survive, he began working on a pig farm. It's hard to imagine a more shameful existence for a Jew than tending unclean animals in a gentile territory and desiring swine food. Coming to his senses, he decided to return to his father, beg forgiveness, and ask to work as a hired servant. This would allow him to pay back what he'd lost and live independently in the village. [68]

Since he violated the community's rule by selling his father's property to gentiles, he would have to face their anger. Returning to the village would be brutal and humiliating, knowing he had to face the gauntlet of insults and hostility.

As he approached the village, word spread and the mob gathered. When the anxious father spotted his son walking toward the gathering crowd, he ran the gauntlet to embrace his offspring.[69] Before the wayward son could voice his prepared speech, his father kissed him and, symbolizing full restoration, ordered his servants to cloak him in his best robe and place a ring on his finger and sandals on his feet.

This public act of reconciliation allowed his son to enter the village under his protective custody. By killing the fatted calf, the whole village could share in this gracious act of forgiveness. [70]

This overwhelming demonstration of love enabled the son to realize the issue was not about lost money, but the broken relationship. This renewed relationship was a pure gift he could never earn—he simply had to accept.[71]

On the other hand, the elder son was expected to attend the banquet, coordinating all hospitality. Instead, he chose to humiliate his father by not attending, creating a major break in their relationship. Ordinarily the father would temporarily ignore this personal insult while hosting his party, but would execute the appropriate punishment later. Instead, he takes the initiative again by searching for his son and begging him to join them. [72]

Claiming moral superiority over his brother, the older son responded to the invite: "Not once did I disobey your orders; yet you never gave me even a young goat to feast on with my friends. But when your son returns who swallowed up your property with prostitutes, for him you slaughter the fatted calf" (Lk.15:29-30).

Like so many religious people (the 99 righteous in the previous parable), the older son demonstrated the attitude of a slave and not a son. "I have worked all my life for you. Where is mine?" In modern language: "I have worshipped regularly, read my Bible daily, said my prayers, contributed to the collections and lived a moral life. Where is my reward?" Remember, he was already given his share of the estate.

The father explained the reason for the celebration: "Your brother was dead and has come back to life again; he was lost and has been found" (Lk.15:32).

The story ends without us knowing if the older brother accepted the father's invitation. All we know is that while the younger brother was feasting, the older sibling was fuming.

In conclusion, the metaphor of this mid-eastern patriarch challenges our understanding of God as lawgiver and judge. It forces us to examine our attitudes toward those we consider morally inferior. It also invites us to open our hearts to unmerited and unlimited love.

Reflection:

1. How do each of the sons speak to you?

2. Which of the father's responses do you find most outlandish and why?

GOOD SAMARITAN (Lk. 10:25-37)

The context of this parable is a lawyer's challenge to Jesus' understanding of the law: Does one inherit eternal life by keeping the law or not? Jesus skillfully avoids the question by asking the questioner to summarize the legal tradition. Condensing the 613 laws of the Torah as loving God (Dt. 6:5) and one's neighbor (Lv. 19:18), Jesus tells him this is the way to eternal life. In an attempt to set some boundaries on this open-ended demand, the lawyer asks for a definition of neighbor. Does it refer to one's tribal relationships, all Jews, or does it also include those converting to the faith? It certainly would not apply to Gentiles.

Jesus responds with the parable of the Samaritan. A man was attacked by robbers and left unconscious and naked on the road. Stripped of any identifying clothing, he was simply a human being in need.

A priest saw the victim and passed by, knowing that if the man was a gentile or dead, he would defile himself if he came within four cubits (17-22 inches) of him. The process of restoring ritual purity was costly and time-consuming. He would be forbidden to collect, distribute or eat the produce given as tithes, resulting in an economic hardship for him and his family. It was more important for him to maintain his status in the community than help the stranger.[73]

The Levite who followed the priest was not bound by as many restrictions. He took a look at the stranger, but also passed by. We don't know his motives, but perhaps he was afraid of the robbers. If the priest passed by, why should he, a mere layman, become involved? "Both the Levite and Priest contributed to the man's suffering by their neglect".[74]

The hero of the story is the Samaritan. He went out of his way to respond to the man in need. He bound his wounds, placed him on his animal (donkey or horse?) and brought him to an inn, and paid for any needed services.

It is difficult for us to imagine a more unlikely hero for a Jewish audience. The Mishnah Shebiith 8:10 states: "He that eats the bread of the Samaritans is liken to one that eats the flesh of swine." Josephus, a Jewish historian, states that this hatred was intensified a few years earlier when Samaritans defiled the Jewish temple during Passover by scattering human bones in the court area.[75]

Jesus demonstrated tremendous courage in telling this story to a Jewish audience. It would be similar to telling a story to our troops of an Isis operative who showed compassion on a wounded American. The word "compassion" and "Isis" just don't fit together in our consciousness. The same dichotomy would apply to "Samaritan" and "neighbor" in first-century Jewish mindfulness. When the lawyer was asked who was a neighbor to the one in need, he couldn't even say "Samaritan." He simply responded: "the one who showed him mercy." Jesus changed the focus from "who is my neighbor?" to "be a neighbor."

The parable challenges us to examine our communal and personal biases toward others. Who are the Samaritans in our lives? How much are we like the priest and Levite trapped by religious rules or fear, preventing us from acting compassionately? The parable reminds us that God's grace can work through unexpected sources. It also teaches us that our neighbor is anyone in need, even an enemy. Finally, the story undermines our illusions of earning our way to heaven. Much like the wounded man, we are all on God's welfare system. We simply have to be humble enough to accept such unexpected love.

Reflection:

1. What religious barriers keep or hinder us from responding to those in need?

2. How does this parable impact your understanding of being a neighbor?

THE PHARISEE AND TAX COLLECTOR
(Lk. 18:9-14)

Jesus tells this parable to a group of people who trusted in their own righteousness and looked upon others with contempt. It reminded me of my Catholic heritage of moral superiority concerning Protestants and members of other religions. The same mindset is prevalent among some Christian traditions who believe that Catholics cannot be saved.

The parable begins with a Pharisee and a tax collector going up to the temple to pray. Dr. Kenneth Bailey, author of *Through Peasant Eyes*, presents a strong argument that the two men were going to attend either the morning (dawn) or 3:00 p.m. atonement ritual when a lamb was sacrificed for the sins of the people. The setting of the parable is communal worship, not private devotion.[76]

Pharisees were deeply religious people who scrupulously attempted to follow the law. Ordinary folks were not well versed in the Torah and the various rules of cleanliness, often rendering them unclean. Conscious of maintaining his ritual purity, the Pharisee stood off by himself, lest he defile himself through physical contact with one of the other worshippers.[77]

After the lamb was sacrificed, the priest would burn incense, allowing worshipers time to express their various petitions and thank God for blessings received. These prayers were usually expressed audibly, and can be experienced today in Jerusalem by standing alongside the Wailing Wall on the Sabbath. The Pharisee used this occasion to teach those around him what it is like to be in the presence of a truly holy man. First of all, he begins by thanking God that he is not like other people: thieves, adulterers or tax collectors. He then informs the others of his virtues. He fasts twice a week, instead of just on the Day of Atonement as required by law (Lv. 25:29; Nm. 39:7). He tithed everything, far surpassing the legal restrictions to just certain items. [78]

The religious exploits of this truly holy man are contrasted sharply with the tax collector, who also stood off by himself, eyes downcast, beating his breast and begging God for mercy. The heartfelt gesture of beating his breast expresses extreme anguish over his failings.[79] True remorse would not only require abandoning his despicable livelihood of collecting taxes for his Roman overseers, but restoring all his dishonest gains. His conversion would severely impact his family.

The parable ends with the two men leaving the temple: the tax collector justified by God's grace, the Pharisee remaining trapped in his illusion of self-righteousness.

The parable, like so many others, reminds us that God's grace cannot be earned, but demands a price. After recognizing his own sinfulness, the tax collector models the humility needed to surrender to the mercy of the Divine Lover. He also demonstrates the courage required to accept God's grace. The story challenges us to examine our attitudes toward those we view with contempt because of their behavior, religious or political beliefs. The truth is that we are all Pharisees in need of surrendering our false sense of self.

Reflection:

1. The Pharisee was considered a holy man because of his fidelity to God's law. What is holiness?

2. What parts of you identify with the main characters in this parable?

RICH MAN AND LAZARUS (Lk. 16:19-31)

This parable is divided into two parts (16:19-26 & 27-31). The context for the story is the belief that wealth and health are blessings from God while poverty and sickness are symptoms of one's sinfulness.

The rich man was extremely wealthy as reflected in his clothes and diet. Dressed in fine purple linen, he ate sumptuously every day, not just on special occasions. His dialogue with Abraham indicates he was aware of Lazarus sitting outside his gate, but he chose to ignore him. His attitude is similar to many today who view poor people as parasites on society, deserving their plight because of laziness and poor choices. Poverty is seen as a personal failure rather than the result of systemic injustice created by a political, legal and an economic system that favors the rich and powerful over those who are powerless.

Lazarus (his name means "God helps") sits outside the rich man's gate longing for the bread used to wipe one's hands after a meal and thrown under the table.[80] Dogs come to lick his exposed wounds.

The parable tells us that in the afterlife their fortunes are totally reversed. Lazarus is reclining in the bosom of Abraham, the place of honor at the heavenly banquet. People in the ancient world believed the saved and sinners could see each other. In an attempt to evoke some privilege as a member of the Jewish faith, the rich man appeals to Abraham to send Lazarus to help relieve his suffering with a drop of water. Many of us feel the same because of our active membership in our various religious traditions. His request is denied because of the inseparable chasm dividing them.

Jesus would have shocked his audience with this reversal of fortunes. "He has put down the mighty from their thrones and raised up those of low degree." (Lk. 1:52). He reminded his listeners that everything belongs to God. We are simply stewards of these resources. Any authentic relationship with God must be translated into a response to any of our brothers or sisters in need. The rich man might have been a faithful worshipper, but prayer without social consequences is simply empty words. As the prophet said: "I hate, I spurn your feasts, I take no pleasure in your solemnities …. If you would offer me holocausts, then let justice surge like water and goodness like and unfailing stream" (Am. 5:21-24).

The rich man requests Abraham to send Lazarus to warn his brothers, the affluent,who are indifferent to the poor. His request is denied. In effect Jesus is telling us that if our lives are not challenged and transformed by the word of God, no great miracle will convince us.

The scriptures have the power to challenge our core beliefs, attitudes and behaviors. Unfortunately, many of us simply read the Bible looking for proof texts to justify our positions or to condemn others with whom we disagree. Scripture reflects the faith journey of our ancestors. It expresses the contradictions, conflicts and paradoxes of their struggle with the Divine in their midst. It is not a substitute for human experience, but a light to illuminate our own faith journey. Unless we enter into a personal struggle with God and the sacred texts, those inspired words will never touch our hearts.

This parable also addresses the widening gap between the rich and the poor throughout the world. So many of the planet's wealthiest people have no regard for the victims created by their greed and abuse of our natural resources. As followers of Jesus, we are challenged to confront the evil of social injustice in accordance with our own economic, social and political status.[81]

Reflection:

1. How does this parable continue to play out today?

2. Who are the Lazaruses at our gates?

THE PENITENT WOMAN (Lk. 7:36-48)

The story takes place at the home of Simon the Pharisee who invited Jesus to dinner. The banquet occurs in the outer courtyard, allowing for uninvited guests to come and listen to the discourse. Meeting at a meal for theological discussion was common practice for religious leaders in the community. The invitation to Jesus and the context of the narrative would indicate they had some concerns about this young sage's teachings.

Those partaking in the meal would recline on one elbow with their legs extended behind them so servants could wash their feet or at least provide the water for purification. Failing to provide this service for Jesus reveals an attitude of superiority, and omitting the greeting kiss was a sign of contempt. It was also a common practice to anoint one's guests with oil. Neglecting these basic rituals of hospitality reflects an attitude of distain for the young rabbi and an attempt to put him in his place. [82]

Witnessing the obvious insult to Jesus, the sinful woman entered the dining area and provided the necessary rituals of hospitality: washing his feet with her tears, drying them with her hair (the letting down of one's hair was an act of intimacy reserved for one's spouse in the context of her home), kissing them and anointing them with the perfumed oil (used by "professional" women to enhance their appeal). [83]

As Simon observed this spectacle, he was convinced Jesus was a false prophet for not recognizing the obvious sinfulness of this woman. Instead of seeing her gestures as an act of love, he judged them to be acts of defilement.

In response, Jesus tells the story of two debtors unable to pay off their loans. Since both debts were forgiven, Simon could understand that the one with the greater debt was more grateful. What he failed to understand was the severity of his own sinfulness. The woman was not a defiling sinner, but one who experienced God's forgiving grace, and was therefore capable of great love. The judgmental Simon became the accused. The drama begins with Jesus under scrutiny and ends with Simon being exposed.

The story reflects a number of theological and psychological insights. God's forgiveness is freely given to all people. This marvelous gift empowers us to love as an expression of our gratitude.[84]Simon represents many of us blinded by religion. Concerned with being morally right, we can no longer see what is good. We classify people according to our beliefs and condemn those who do not live up to our standards. In the patriarchal setting, women were inferior to men and had no identity outside of marriage or motherhood. Widows or single women were often forced into prostitution for economic survival. This story depicts a despised woman as a heroine of faith. Jesus undermines all gender bias by reaching out to women throughout his ministry. God's love is often manifested in the lives of people once considered sinful. Like Simon, we will never understand unless we walk that journey. Compassion and forgiveness are usual qualities of one who has been there.

Reflection:

    1. Identify the Simon within yourself.

    2. How has God's forgiveness freed you to become more loving?

THE GREAT BANQUET (Lk. 14:1-24)

Jesus addressed this parable to those who were gathered with him for the Sabbath meal in the home of one of the leading Pharisees. Challenging their Sabbath protocols by healing a man with dropsy, he continued his confrontation with observations about his fellow guests seeking places of honor at the table. He also suggested his host should invite the poor to his meals instead of his friends, relatives or wealthy neighbors. Jesus began his parable in response to a fellow guest referencing the joy of the heavenly banquet.

In order to fully appreciate the story, it is important to realize that in the cultural context of the time, two invitations were sent. The first stated the date and time of the banquet. The number of those who accepted determined the size of the menu. A chicken was served if only four people responded, but a calf was prepared if the guest list was near seventy. The parable indicates that the host expected a large amount of people. When the meal was prepared, the master sent his servant to inform those invited that dinner was ready. All those invited began to excuse themselves for various reasons.[85]

The first man lied by claiming he bought a field and had to go and inspect it. No one ever bought land without knowing every inch of it, including its history of production.[86]

The second man also lied, stating he bought oxen and had to go and test them. No one ever bought oxen without first seeing how they worked together as a team. The animals were only sold after being tested.[87]

The third man claimed he just got married and had to spend time with his wife. In a patriarchal culture, using a woman to avoid social obligation was the ultimate insult. First of all, the host would never have competed with a village wedding by scheduling his banquet near the same time. Secondly, banquets were usually held in the late afternoon, so there would have been plenty of time in the evening to attend to his wife's needs. Finally, this guest didn't even bother to excuse himself; he simply stated that he could not come.[88]

Though deeply insulted by the rejection, the host, however, responded graciously, not angrily. He invited the poor, blind and lame: all those living in the village but considered outside of the community.

Since there was still room at the banquet, the master sent his servant outside the village to the highways and hedges to compel anyone he found to come. A total stranger to the village would never believe such a gracious gift. The servant would have to take the startled person by the arm and pull him along. [89]

Jesus used this parable to confront the Pharisees and Lawyers who could not accept open table fellowship. The banquet is the messianic banquet that ushers in a new age. The original guests were the leaders of Israel who simply refused the invitation. The strangers outside the village were the gentiles.

The parable reminds us that we are all invited to the heavenly banquet. Our God does not reject anyone, but we have a choice to either accept or refuse such an extraordinary gift.

It also exposes our attitudes toward those we think unworthy: non-Christians, public sinners, gays and even politicians. The complete text forces us to critique our liturgical meals that are often reserved only for those deemed worthy.

Reflection:

1. What excuses have we used to distance ourselves from our Divine Host?

2. Who are the outsiders in our worldview?

LABORERS IN THE VINEYARD (Mt. 20:1-15)

One of the most challenging parables is the story of the laborers in the vineyard. In its original context, Jesus was probably addressing the religious leaders, his most vocal critics.

The story begins with the owner hiring laborers at the break of dawn to work his vineyard. He agrees to pay them a denarius, the usual wage for a day's work. The owner goes out again at nine, noon and three o'clock. He goes out a final time at five and still finds people in need of work.

When the workday was finished at six, the owner called the workers together, beginning with those last hired, to pay them their wages. When they received a full day's wage, those hired first assumed they would receive more. However, after receiving the exact same amount as agreed upon when hired, they complained bitterly.

To appreciate the full impact of this parable, place yourself in the story as among those first hired and enduring the heat of the sun throughout the day. When those who worked only one hour received the same recompense, it wasn't right. Our sense of fairness has been violated—that is the point of the story.

We are challenged to examine the source of our anger. The issue is not the seeming injustice of the story. Rather, the parable uncovers the fact that our sense of value comes from our comparison with others. I am "somebody" in relation to you because I am better than you: morally, physically, intellectually and socially. We have a vested interest in the perceived inferiority of others. The owner's generosity is the last thing we want, because it equalizes everything. It takes away our sense of merit and privilege.

Our anger is a symptom of having our competitiveness and envy exposed. Our pseudo identity has emerged over years by playing such a game. God's generous love undermines the whole system and challenges us to examine who we really are. Is my inherent worth based on my comparison to others or on the Divine Presence at the core of my being?

Reflection:

1. How does this parable confront your sense of fairness?

2. How has competition and comparison impacted our forma-
   tional identity?

PAUL

Paul is one of the most controversial figures in the history of Western civilization. Some claim that Christianity would not have survived without him; others believe that he distorted the teachings of Jesus. His writings and life have evoked debates about the role of women in the church, slavery, homosexuality, our attitude toward government authority and the role of the Jewish tradition in Christianity. Pauline texts have been used to justify violence and oppression throughout the history of Christianity. For better or worse, he inspired such religious leaders as Augustine (original sin), Luther (faith vs. works), Calvin (pre-destination) and Wesley (personal salvation).

Our knowledge of Paul comes primarily from his letters. As a secondary source, the Book of Acts, revealing his role in the spread of Christianity, needs to be critically evaluated, since Luke was writing as a theologian, not a historian.

Paul was born and raised in Tarsus, a prosperous commercial center known for its Stoic and Epicurean schools of philosophy. His letters reflect a fluency in Greek, rhetorical techniques, a brilliant mind, strong personality and the spirituality of a mystic. He was born a Jew, educated as a Pharisee and transformed into a follower of Jesus.

"Circumcised on the eighth day of the race of Israel of the tribe of Benjamin, a Hebrew of Hebrew parentage, in observance of the law a Pharisee, in zeal I persecuted the church, in righteousness based on the law I was blameless" (Phil: 3:5-6).

As a Pharisee, Paul believed in angelic beings and life after death. He not only revered the Torah (first five books of the Bible), but the oral tradition adapting the covenant laws to changing circumstances. Paul persecuted the early Christian Jews for proclaiming that a crucified insurrectionist was the messiah, contradicting the sacred text: "God's curse rests on him who hangs on a tree…" (Dt. 21:23).

In reading Paul there are a number of issues to keep in mind.

1. Although he was born about the same time, he did not know Jesus in the flesh. He experienced the risen Lord while traveling the road to Damascus with written orders to persecute followers of the "Way."

2. When Paul wrote his letters there was no New Testament. The scriptures were the Greek version (Septuagint) of the Old Testament.

3. He did not intend to write scripture. He was writing to Christian communities to explain his theology or respond to local issues that were undermining the solidarity of its members. His letters were circulated among the churches and eventually gathered together in the first third of the second century. We do not have all of the letters he wrote, and most scholars claim that several of the epistles that bear his name were written after his death.

4. Paul had a communal sense of reality. Any notion of personal or private salvation would be foreign to him.

5. Paul liked to set up a problem in terms of antithesis or paradoxes, but he was primarily a dialectical thinker. He did not view reality as divided, but synthesized because of the Christ event. "In Jesus there is no Jew or Greek, slave or free, male or female; all are one in Christ."

6. Paul was not a Christian, as we understand the term today. He was a Jew who believed that Jesus was the expected messiah. He did not intend to break with his religious past, but transform it.

7. The primary issue facing the Pauline churches was, "How Jewish does a Christian have to be?" There were those who insisted on full observance of Jewish law, including circumcision. Another group did not demand circumcision,

but required converted Gentiles to keep all the dietary and other laws. Paul belonged to a third group who discounted the kosher laws, but refrained from eating food sacrificed to idols. They also expected fellow believers to observe the major Jewish holidays. The final group basically discounted all of the Jewish tradition except the Ten Commandments. [90]

8. Paul was strongly influenced by the apocalyptic expectations of his day. His belief that Christ was returning in glory during his lifetime strongly influenced his attitudes about marriage, virginity and his compulsion to spread the Gospel throughout the Roman Empire.

Reflection:

1. What are your feelings about Paul?

2. How would Paul fit into today's church?

HISTORICAL CONTEXT

Paul lived in the context of the Greco-Roman world comprising the lands stretching from England to Syria, including Egypt and North Africa. Since the time of Alexander the Great (300 BCE), Greek language and culture impacted commerce, religion, community and family systems. People defined themselves in terms of group membership, not as individuals. As an honor and shame-based ethos, respect was due to wealth, education, rhetorical skill, family pedigree and political connections; self-esteem was based on the acceptance or rejection of one's family, peers and socioeconomic group. [91]

It was a hierarchical system similar to the domination systems of ancient Egypt at the time of Moses and Solomon's Israel. Power was concentrated in the hands of the emperor and the top 5% of the wealthiest citizens. Supporting this governing class were the religious and political bureaucrats who attended to the needs of the elite and maintained the daily functioning of government. The merchants, possessing some wealth but little or no political power, were next in line. They were followed by the slaves, who acted as middle managers for the elite. The next lower level consisted of artisans, free day-laborers (working poor) and lower-level slaves. At the bottom of the pyramid were the unclean and expendables such as widows, orphans and disabled.[92]

As a patriarchal society, the male head of the household governed his little universe, treating his wife, children and slaves as personal property. Unwanted babies were often dumped on a garbage heap to die or be retrieved as slaves or prostitutes. Women were generally relegated to the home as wives, mothers and household managers. Aristocratic women were often educated and wielded a great deal of political, economic and religious influence.[93]

Slavery was a well-established economic institution throughout the Greco-Roman world. Slavery was not racially based, but the result of conquest, piracy, abandonment, debt repayment or birth, as was common during Paul's lifetime. Slaves possessed few legal rights and were considered property to be used or abused according to the desires of their masters. Some slaves rose to prominence by learning a trade and managing their master's business. Some were freed by their masters to demonstrate generosity or were released at the time of their owner's death as a reward for faithful service. [94]

In 27 BCE, Octavian Caesar defeated the armies of Mark Antony and Cleopatra in the Battle of Actium, bringing an end to a long period of civil strife and inaugurating a period of peace lasting about 200 years. Upon his triumphal entry into Rome, the senate bestowed on him the title Augustus (Divine One), initiating a litany of accolades reflected in literature and worship throughout the empire: Prince of Peace, Lord, Son of God, Redeemer, Liberator and Savior of the World. The confluence of religion, politics and military power begat the "Pax Romana" or Roman Peace brought about through conquest, subjugation and intimidation. The people brought under Roman rule were forced to pay tribute in exchange for services rendered: protection, good roads, uniform legal and monetary systems.[95] Those who refused to comply or rebelled were crucified, a form of capital punishment perfected by the Romans.

Religion played a significant role throughout the empire. Reflecting an openness and tolerance for various practices, polytheism, the worship of many gods, was common. Beside the great pantheon of Jupiter, Mars and Venus, or their Greek equivalents, there existed a hierarchy of gods descending from state, city and household to numerous lesser divinities. At the bottom of the pyramid were alleged progenies of divine and human intercourse such as Caesar Augustus, Hercules, Plato or Apollonius of Tyana, who was miraculously born, worked miracles, died and rose again to be with the other gods. [96]

As an expression of their loyalty and patriotism, everyone except the Jews was required to worship the state gods, often a depiction of Caesar to be honored with the burning of incense. The Jews were exempt because Rome respected the antiquity of their religious beliefs.

Ancient religions focused on ritual practices not dogmatic beliefs or moral behavior. Ethics was a philosophical not a religious concern. Religion for most people was a means of securing favors from the gods during their lifetime, since they did not believe in the afterlife.[97]

Evangelizing in the context of the Greco-Roman world, Paul's gospel of a crucified-resurrected Savior challenged the political, economic, religious and social systems that reinforced the Pax Romana. His message, much like his Master's, proved to be treasonous.

Questions for reflection:

1. How is the Pax Romana similar and different from Pax Americana?

2. What lessons can we learn from Paul's world?

PAULINE LITERATURE

In Paul's letters "there are some things hard to understand that the ignorant and unstable distort to their own destruction, just as they do the other scriptures" (2 Pt. 3:16).

The New Testament attributes thirteen letters to Paul. Mainline scholars are almost unanimous in their opinion that Paul wrote seven of these: 1 Thessalonians (49-50), Galatians, 1 Corinthians, Philemon, Philippians, 2 Corinthians, and Romans (59-60). Pauline authorship of 2 Thessalonians is still heavily debated. Most scholars agree that Colossians (80s), Ephesians (90s) were written one or two generations after Paul, who died around 64. Scholars are also unanimous in the opinion that 1&2 Timothy and Titus (100-110) were not written by Paul.

Paul's original letters reflect a radical egalitarianism which becomes more hierarchical and patriarchal in succeeding generations. As the church became more institutionalized, it adapted to the values of the Greco/Roman culture.[98]

Paul deals with the issue of slavery in his letter to Philemon. Reflecting his theology that economic, gender and social differences disappear for those baptized in Christ (Gal. 3:27-28), he argues that Onesimus, the runaway slave who helped Paul in prison and was baptized, is now equal to his owner, Philemon, and should be treated accordingly. In the second generation of letters (Col. 3:22-4:1) slaves are told to obey their masters and masters are told to treat their slaves justly. In the third generation of letters slaves are told it is God's will that they respect their masters by providing good service... No advice is given to the masters in regard to slaves (1Tm. 6:1-2).[99]

Concerning women, the radical Paul shows the same egalitarian regard. In his letter to the Romans he greets a number of women and refers to Junia as an apostle in ministry before him. He sends Phoebe, a deacon, to deliver and explain his letter to the Romans. He takes women prophets in the Corinthian community (1Cor. 11:5) and female leadership at Philippi (Phil. 4:2-3) for granted.[100]

There is a passage in his Corinthian correspondence about women remaining silent in church and seeking knowledge from their husbands (1Cor. 14:34-35). This text did not appear in the earliest manuscripts and was a footnote in later ones, eventually making its way into the manuscript. It also contradicts the passage noted above that recognizes women prophets.[101]

In his first letter to the Corinthians, Paul argues for mutuality in marriage. The second generation of letters tells women to be obedient to their husbands and husbands to love their wives like Christ loves the church (Eph: 5:21-32). The third generation of letters tells women they are forbidden to teach men and to ask their husbands if they want to learn anything. Their salvation is in bearing children (1Tm: 2:11-15).[102]

It is quite apparent from these examples that as the church went from a charismatic model guided by the Spirit to a hierarchical model, it began to express the economic, gender and social status reflected in society, and lost the egalitarian radicalism of the original Paul.

Questions for reflection:

1. How does separating the authentic Pauline letters from the others impact your understanding of him?

2. How does the Church reflect our cultural values and how does it differ?

THE POWER OF SIN

I grew up with an understanding that sin was any thought, desire, word, deed or omission contrary to the law of God. A mortal sin was a grievous offense done knowingly and willingly, and deprived a person of grace and made one an enemy of God. A venial sin was a lesser offense that did not destroy one's relationship with our Creator. Sin was viewed as a personal and private behavioral response to a set of divinely established laws. It was understood in the context of a performance-based religious structure.

Paul would have understood such a meritorious system because of his Pharisaical background and his knowledge of the Torah. However, his experience on the way to Damascus expanded his consciousness about God and our failure to live up to our calling as Divine sons and daughters.

Paul's encounter challenged him with fundamental questions: How could he have done such evil in the name of following the divinely revealed law? How could he have been so blinded by his religious fervor that he could not see the goodness of the followers of The Way? How could his perception of reality have been so distorted that he totally missed the mark (*harmatia*, his Greek term for "sin")?

As Paul meditated on these issues, he began to view the role of Mosaic Law in a totally different context from his training. The Law was held in such high respect that some, thinking that God studied the Torah daily, believed God and the Law were inseparable. [103]

Paul began to see that the Law provided information, but it could not lead to transformation. Like many of his contemporaries, he had defined himself in terms of a thing. By focusing his gaze on the Torah, Paul lost sight of reality. He began to understand that the Law was a guide to adulthood, but excessive respect for it resulted in perpetual immaturity and external religious observances. The history of the Jewish people and the distorted perception of human nature indicated that sin had to be something greater than the failure to live up to the requirements of the Law. [104]

As Paul meditated on the etiology of evil in the Genesis story of Adam and Eve, he became convinced that their refusal to live as children of the Creator set in motion a power that enslaved us all.

The old Adam became his metaphor for sinful humanity. Adam's choice to live independently of God initiated a massive disorientation of society that manifests itself in divisiveness, violence, greed, sexual exploitation, dishonesty and the misuse of power.

Paul sees sin as rejection of the humanity for which we were created. It is alienation from God, others, creation and our true selves. It is living a life of self-deception. It is the power or force that controls human behavior and pervades human existence.

Paul believes sin is an expression of a dualistic consciousness that permeates our environment and perpetuates our divisions. It is the condition of humanity that traps all people, Jews and Gentiles alike (Rom. 3:9). The values of a disoriented society enslave everyone from generation to generation. The dynamics that seem to be directing humankind on the path of evil is the cumulative effect of a multitude of individual decisions over centuries. Sin is the inexorable pressure of a false-value system that pervades the world.[105]

In a society that puts a premium on independence and self-sufficiency, everything concurs to impress the individual with the desirability of these attitudes. In a society that measures status by material possessions, everyone desires far more than what they need. In a society that glorifies youth and appearances, billions are spent on surgeries, Botox, lotions and brand name clothes. In a society that respects power, military budgets go unquestioned while services to the poor and needy are characterized as wasteful handouts. In a society that idolizes unbridled capitalism, the environment is simply a resource to be exploited regardless of the long term consequences. The list could go on, but the accepted value system of our way of life exercises a tremendous pressure on anyone who tries to hold out against it. The prevailing mindset and attitudes of our culture could not possibly be distorted, and those who think differently are often held up to ridicule. Only the very strong can offer any resistance. Most people simply comply and are not even conscious of how they are being manipulated.

Paul believes that we were created with free will. However, the power of sin that permeates the world makes it impossible to exercise that freedom without divine intervention. Speaking on behalf of humanity, Paul states: "What I do, I do not understand. For I do not do what I want, but what I hate… For I do not do the good I want, but I do the evil I do not want. If I do what I do not want, it is no longer I who do it but sin that dwells in me… Miserable one that I am! Who will deliver me from this mortal body? Thanks be to God through Jesus Christ our Lord" (Rm. 7:15-25).

Reflection:

1. How does Paul's notion of sin differ from yours?

2. Why is covetousness such a powerful force in our present culture?

THE NEW ADAM

"For just as through one man's sin entered the world and with sin death… For if by the offense of the one man all died, much more did the grace of God and the gracious gift of the one man, Jesus Christ, abound for all… Just as a single offense brought condemnation to all men, a single righteous act brought all men acquittal and life" (Rm. 5:12, 16, 20).

Unfortunately, Augustine used this passage to support his doctrine of Original Sin, believing Adam's guilt was passed on to succeeding generations through the procreative act. This doctrine not only painted God as an unforgiving judge, it alienated men and women from themselves and their sexuality. Nothing could be further from Paul's intent.

Paul views religious history in four stages: 1, humanity before the fall; 2, humanity from Adam's rebellion to the Covenant with the Israelites; 3, life under the Mosaic Law, which revealed the continued enslavement to sin; and 4, humanity after the coming of Christ. Jesus was for Paul what Adam was destined to be and what the Torah failed to accomplish. Because Adam failed to live in obedience to his calling as God's son, all of humanity became enslaved by sin. Jesus was the one who remained faithful to his calling, even to his death, thus freeing us from our bondage.

Jesus entered fully into our humanity. His temptations throughout his life, recorded in Matthew (Ch. 4) and Luke (Ch. 4), reflected the same powers and forces that entrap us in a false sense of self. Unlike the first Adam, Jesus remained true to his calling as God's son, revealing an option other than enslavement to sin—a life lived in accordance with Original Blessing. We are not permanently flawed. If one could maintain his authenticity despite the forces to the contrary, all could become free.[106]

Paul's master story was an early Christian hymn (Phil. 2:6-8) proclaiming Jesus' humiliation and exaltation. Unlike Adam, who attempted to exalt himself, Jesus' death epitomized his life of total self-giving, modeling for Paul and his communities the consequences of love. [107]

Jesus' death was not preordained according to some divine mandate that required a price to be paid for human sinfulness. He saw the destruction caused by the religious, political, economic and social structures, and responded out of a deep compassion for those victimized. Those empowered by the false value systems could not control him, so they had to kill him.

Jesus entered fully into our humiliation even to the point where his death was considered a curse in Jewish tradition (Dt. 21:23). However, his death was not an ending, but the beginning of a new way of living. God raised him from the dead, and thus revealed the primary pattern of all of reality. "For this reason God exalted him and bestowed on him the name that is above every name, that at the name of Jesus every knee should bend and every tongue confess that Jesus Christ is Lord to the glory of God the Father" (Phil. 2:9-11).

God, in effect, looked upon our sinful orientation and passed judgment. "You are all acquitted! You will always be my sons and daughters, and I love you. My son has now revealed what it means to be authentically human. I now empower you with His spirit to live transformed lives." This, for Paul, was the gospel.

Justification is not something we do. It is what God does for us in Jesus. The core of religion is not about performance, knowing correct creeds or following a set of legal prescriptions, but participating in the process of dying and rising. "Christ died for all that those who live might live no longer for themselves, but for him who for their sake died and was raised... therefore if anyone is in Christ he/she is a new creation; the old things have passed away; they have become new" (2Cor 5:15-17).

Paul believed that Jesus was the expected Messiah. Defying the expectations of his day, Jesus came as a Suffering Servant as described in Isaiah, not as a King, High Priest or the Teacher of Righteousness. He showed us that the way to power was through powerlessness, success through failure and salvation through our sinfulness. The way to glory was through disappointment, not achievement. Paul reminds us that because of Christ's death, history is inherently optimistic. What we destroy, God renews.

For Paul, Christ is both the promise and goal of humanity. He is the one who has begun the process of reconciling the opposites created by human sinfulness, uniting the human with the divine, the material with the spiritual, male with the female, the now with eternity. In Him, we are now empowered to hold together the contradictions in our own lives. In Him we are all equal, regardless of socio-economic or religious status.

Paul saw in Christ a new vision of what we could and should become. Jesus showed us the way to live authentically. He was convinced that he was not proposing a utopian ideal because Jesus actually lived the life God intended for Adam. [108] He realized that in order for us to follow the example of Jesus, we needed to surrender to His love and be empowered by His Spirit. We needed to embrace our Original Blessing.

Reflection:

1. How does beginning life as Original Blessing or Original Sin impact our self-perception and view of God?

2. What does it mean to live authentically?

FLESH VS. SPIRIT

"Those who live according to the flesh are intent on the things of the flesh; those who live according to the spirit, on those of the spirit. The tendency of the flesh is toward death, but that of the spirit toward life and peace. The flesh in its tendency is at enmity with God… those who are in the flesh cannot please God" (Rm. 8: 5-8).

Paul uses Flesh and Spirit to connote two modes of existence, which he characterizes as death and life. Flesh, reflecting his negative value judgment on the quality of human existence, refers to humanity living under the power of sin. [109]

Flesh is living out of a false sense of self. Our modern day term would be the Ego. It reflects an inauthentic existence contrary to our original calling as sons and daughters of a loving parent. To some degree all of us are enslaved by our egos.

The process of developing an identity takes the first thirty to forty years of our lives. During this time we internalize our reactions to our successes and failures, the acceptance or rejection of significant people and our comparison with others. Family, friends, church, civic organizations and country validate and enhance our false selves. Throughout this process we are restricted by our ego's need to be in control, to be right, to look good and to define ourselves in relationship to others. It is a necessary process, but one that distorts our perceptions, perpetuates divisions and limits our possibilities.

Paul is reminding us that who we are has nothing to do with accomplishments, power, prestige, possessions, appearances or the opinions of others. Those values simply reflect the power of sin in our lives. Living according to the Flesh leaves us needy, insecure and filled with false desires. It is not so much an evil, but often manifests itself through destructive behaviors: "lewd conduct, impurity, licentiousness, idolatry, sorcery, hostilities, bickering, jealousy, outbursts of rage, selfish rivalries, dissensions, factions, envy, drunkenness, orgies and the like" (Gal. 5:19-20).

Our Spirit self is who we are in God. We are children of the Creator who loves us unconditionally—it is simply a gift

Paul reminds us that our truest self is divine. We are spiritual beings who must learn how to become authentically human. When we die to our ego consciousness and are born again into our Spirit consciousness as ritualized in Baptism, we begin to realize that each of our lives are part of a much bigger story. We are called to participate with our Creator in the much greater process of reconciliation. Our role is to enter into union with ourselves, others and creation. *Shalom* is the Hebrew word for the experience of being connected. This dying process usually occurs after our forties.

The world can no longer be broken down simplistically into me and you, we and they, good and bad or saints and sinners as viewed through our ego consciousness. Either we are all children of God or no one is. Either we are all human or none of us are. Either all are part of creation or nothing is. The false divisions that separate us from others, our environment or ourselves are ego-controlled criteria that perpetuates these enmities in order to maintain our false identity and assumptions about life.

When empowered by the Spirit, we literally become a new creation manifesting a life of "love, joy, peace, patient endurance, kindness, generosity, faith, mildness and chastity" (Gal. 5:22-23). Religion becomes an experience of joy rather than one of duty. We no longer have to prove ourselves to God. God has come to us. Life in the Spirit frees us to be non-judgmental, compassionate, forgiving and mystical, allowing us to view reality through a unitive consciousness. Life in the Spirit means living as God intended us to be.

The process is never fully completed, and, for many people, rarely initiated. However, as one begins to internalize the baptismal ritual of dying and rising, there are moments that draw us into deeper realities we can only describe as divine experiences of being fully alive and at home in the very core of our being.

Reflection:

1. How would you describe your false sense of self?
2. When have you felt most your true self?

THE BODY OF CHRIST

"Saul, Saul, why are you persecuting me?" was the key revelation that haunted Paul. He understood that if Christ identified in a mystical bodily manner with His people, it was essential for him to strategically establish communities throughout the Roman Empire. He selected Thessalonica, Philippi, Corinth and Ephesus because they were the major centers for trade and commerce. Galatia referred to the region where Paul and Barnabas founded a number of communities of Celtic ancestry on his first missionary journey.

Paul's strategy was to establish stable communities consisting of 25 to 50 people who accepted the Lordship of Jesus, and demonstrated a new way of living and relating to each other. The churches were missionary in nature, proclaiming the Gospel of a crucified savior and reaching out to the needs of the poor, widowed, orphaned and forgotten of society. Membership included people from all levels of society with the majority from the lower economic strata. Men and women participated in ministry as apostles, teachers, prophets, healers or administrators according to the gifts of the Spirit.

Although Paul attempted to reach out to his fellow Hebrews, he was more successful with those of a Gentile background who were attracted to and supportive of the Jewish traditions. Many of these "God-fearers," after hearing the news about Jesus, chose to become Christian rather than Jew, creating great animosity toward Paul within the Jewish communities. [110]

Paul's most succinct description of the church is found in his letter to the Galatians: "All of you who have been baptized into Christ have clothed yourselves with him. There does not exist among you Jew or Greek, slave or freeman, male or female. All are one in Christ Jesus. (3:27-29)." [111]

Paul realized that in order to free us from the destructive value system of society, he needed to establish an alternative environment that would provide inspiration and support on our journey to authenticity. His code phrases for this new reality were: "belonging to Christ," "putting on Christ" and "in Christ," which he uses 155 times.

For Paul, the church reflected Christ's ongoing presence in our midst. One didn't join the church in the sense of signing a membership form. You entered by participating in the paschal mystery of dying to one's false self and rising conscious of being a son or daughter of God. Members no longer had to compete with each other, but could support one another, "Beloved, clothe yourselves with heartfelt mercy, with kindness, humility, meekness and patience. Bear with one another; forgive each other just as the Lord has forgiven you. Over all these virtues, put on love, which binds the rest together and makes them perfect. Christ's peace must reign in your hearts, since as members of the one body you have been called to that peace" (Col. 3:12-15).

Because of the transformative power of such fellowship, the early Christians had a positive sense of identity and described themselves as the communion of saints. Emboldened by such a communal force, they were able to reach out to others, even their enemies (Rm. 12:20-21).

Paul understood that Faith was not just surrender to the Lordship of Jesus, but a choice for a communal way of living and a commitment to a life of self-giving. He would never have understood our present day notion of personal salvation and privatized religion. He viewed individualism as a characteristic of inauthenticity. The Greek word for such an existence is idiotos (idiot). Since we were created in the image of God, our basic vocation is to love. "If I possess all of the charisms of the Spirit, have faith strong enough to move mountains and give everything I have to the poor, but do not have love, I am nothing" (1Cor. 13:1-3). Love is faith in action.

Referring to the forces of a false value-laden society as Powers and Principalities (Rm. 8:38), Paul understood our vulnerability as individuals. Only the communal force of love can empower its members to become their true selves. When Paul responds to the numerous issues that plagued the local churches, his overriding concern was maintaining the solidarity of its members. The good of the community took precedence over individual rights. The truest expression of freedom was to refrain from exercising one's legitimate rights out of concern for the greater good. In other words, true freedom is freedom from the tyranny of the self, which plagues our present society. Living in a country that glorifies the individual, we are trapped more than ever in a false sense of self and a dualistic consciousness that perpetuates our divisions. Paul's vision of church also became distorted, succumbing to the hierarchical and patriarchal forces of the Greco/Roman culture.

The journey to authenticity begins by loving one other person who mirrors back to us our true and false self, opening us to others in an ever inclusive dynamic. Once we become convinced that community is the basic Christian reality, we will commit ourselves to strengthening our primary relationships, local parishes or forming small base communities.

Reflection:

1. What forces are undermining your growth toward authenticity?

2. Describe any communal experience that has promoted your authenticity.

EUCHARIST

"I received from the Lord what I also handed on to you, that the Lord Jesus, on the night he was handed over, took bread, and after he had given thanks, broke it and said, 'This is my body that is for you. Do this in remembrance of me.' In the same way also the cup, after supper saying, 'This is the new covenant in my blood, do this as often as you drink it, in remembrance of me.'"

Paul received this ritual tradition from Christ through His Body in Antioch. The Lord's communal presence was the basis of Paul's understanding of Eucharist. Contrary to later traditions that began to focus on the bread, wine and words of institution, Paul gave primacy to the communal gathering.

At issue in Corinth was the scandalous behavior of some member who modeled the Eucharist according to the social stratification manifesting itself in civil society. Sanctioning such practices in their Eucharistic gatherings, the upper class enjoyed better quality food and drink, and were often well satiated and inebriated before the poorer members could leave work to join them, having to settle for the remnants of what was left.

Paul challenged this behavior by saying this was not Eucharist. Even though the words of institution were spoken, it was not Christ speaking them, because the Lord was not present in such a divided community. Paul's message was clear: consecrated bread and wine are an empty, powerless sacrament without loving, supportive relationships.[112]

By shifting the focus to the consecrated bread and wine, the Eucharistic gatherings have lost the dynamic transformative power originally intended. The simple gesture of eating and drinking regardless of social status, age, gender or ideology is a radical counter-cultural symbol proclaiming who we are as members of

God's family. This is why restrictions based on worthiness, religion or marital status are so destructive, undermining the gospel of God's justice, mercy and compassion.

By shifting the focus back to the community, the action of eating and drinking expands the sacrament to everyday life. When families gather for the holidays reveling in the joy of being together, it is Eucharist. When friends gather for pasta and wine, sharing what's happening in their lives, it is Eucharist. When hunting partners gather at camp enjoying the fruits of their labors, bonding over past exploits and failures, it is Eucharist. When brothers gather by a lake cooking fish over an open fire and sharing family memories, it is Eucharist. When you help in a soup kitchen or gather for fellowship in a church hall, you are participating in Eucharist. When you bring lasagna to a grieving family, or food to an elderly couple, you are bringing Eucharist. When you make love to your significant other, it is Eucharist. Eucharist is communion, the experience of being connected, reminding us that all of reality shares the same life force.

It is precisely the communal dimension of sharing a meal that was at the heart of Jesus' ministry. "This man welcomes sinners and eats with them" (Lk. 15:2). "He is a glutton and a drunkard" (Lk. 7:34). His words in response to all of this: "Do this in memory of me" — this is Eucharist!

Questions for reflection:

   1. How does Paul's understanding of Eucharist differ from yours?

   2. Describe Eucharistic experiences you have had outside of the official liturgical ritual.

BOOK OF REVELATION

The Book of Revelation, a.k.a. Apocalypse, is the most contro-versial and difficult section of the Bible to interpret. Throughout history this strange and mysterious piece of literature has been used to condemn others, predict the end of the world, invent peculiar doc-trines and form strange sects. Understanding the meaning of the book requires knowledge of its historical context and familiarity with apocalyptic genre.

The text was written around 95(CE) when Domitian was emperor of Rome. The author identifies himself as a certain "John," who was exiled to the small rocky island of Patmos in the Aegean Sea between Greece and Asia Minor (modern day Turkey). John may have been a traveling prophet who visited the various Christian communities that he addressed in his writing. He was well versed in the Old Testament and was probably a Jew who converted to Christianity. He may have been affiliated with the Ephesians who gave us the Fourth Gospel. His strong antipathy toward Rome also suggests he may have wit-nessed the destruction of Jerusalem and the temple.[113]

Writing as a prophet confronting the Greco-Roman system, John claims his message is a direct revelation from God. He challenged the underlying values imbedded in the fabric of everyday living: greed, violence, injustice and sexual promiscuity. The early Chris-tians were involved in a culture war not unlike our own.

He also encouraged his fellow Christians to defy Rome's underlying religious underpinnings. Although tolerant of local religions, the regional governors were anxious to guarantee loyalty to the empire, requiring people of all religions to pay tribute to the Roman gods as a sign of their loyalty. Emperor worship was common during Domitian's

reign. This ritual usually required spilling some wine, a so-called liba-
tion offering, and casting a pinch of incense on the altar fire before
Caesar's image. The practice was seen less as an affirmation of religious faith than a gesture of civic virtue, not unlike the recital of the
Pledge of Allegiance in contemporary American classrooms. However,
any citizen who refused to participate was suspected of disloyalty, if
not outright treason. [114]

The Jews were excused because of the antiquity of their religion.
Since Christianity was relatively new, members, depending on the
local magistrate, often had to choose between the Lordship of Jesus
and Caesar.

In order to survive in the Roman world, the followers of Jesus constantly faced choices that impacted them financially, socially and
spiritually. John was a rigid cultural warrior similar to those today
who strongly oppose the secular destruction of Judeo-Christian values. He condemned other Christian prophets for advocating any
compromise with such an evil milieu, and advised his faithful readers to remain patient and passive, even if it meant imprisonment, torture and death. He condemned those who handled Roman coins
because they were imprinted with the image of the "divine" Caesar.
[115]

John's prophetic work was put in the form of a letter to seven
churches in Asia Minor. He used a literary genre not familiar to us,
but common to the people of his day. The style of writing probably
originated in Persia, modern-day Iran, which had a sophisticated
angiology consisting of good and evil spirits. Apocalyptic literature
in Israel developed around the year 200 (BCE) in response to the
oppressive practices of Antiochus IV, who attempted to destroy the
Jewish religion. The prophetic tradition, interpreting evil as God's
response to covenant disobedience, could not account for the massive suffering the Jewish people experienced under Antiochus.

The author of the Book of Daniel and John of Patmos viewed their
oppression by the Syrians and Romans respectively as a cosmic
struggle between God and Satan. The revelation John imparted to his
readers was that God wins. His people may suffer persecution at the

hands of the wicked, but God is always victorious over evil. Just as Jesus conquered death, so will those who remain faithful. Through their sufferings they will enter into Jesus' own glory, and live with him forever in the new and eternal Jerusalem. Like a great symphonic theme, this revelation will be repeated throughout the book.

Beside the Book of Daniel and passages in the Gospels (Mk. 13:14-27) describing the end times, there are numerous apocalyptic writings that do not appear in the Bible, such as the First Book of Enoch, the Apocalypse of Abraham, the Testament of the Patriarch and the Book of Jubilees.

The language of apocalyptic literature is designed for the right brain. Unlike left-brain writing that is rational, logical and analytical, apocalyptic language is richly symbolic. Numbers, persons, places, animals, actions, objects and parts of the body are used to convey conceptual images. The symbols are not to be taken literally, but are intended to leave us with an impression or an idea. For example, when someone says that New York is a jungle, we do not expect to see vines and untamed animals. We automatically interpret the image as portraying a wild, chaotic city.

Most of the descriptions used by the author come directly from the Old Testament. Of the 404 verses in the Book of Revelation, there are over 500 allusions to the Old Testament. Most of the metaphors can easily be interpreted, but there are some requiring an educated guess.

During the next five meditations, I will try to hit the highlights of the book and hopefully convey the powerful message that John intended for his readers. For those who feel powerless and vulnerable, his revelation is one of hope and consolation.

There are several points to keep in mind while reading the Book of Revelation.

1. The text was framed in the form of a letter, and was sent to the various churches of Asia Minor (modern day Turkey) to be read out loud when the assembly gathered for worship. I would recommend reading the content out loud in

the privacy of your home to get the full benefit of all the images and symbols.

2. The Book does not predict events that are happening in our day. John is addressing the Christians at the end of the first century. However, his message is meta-historical, applying to people of all ages.

3. The author addresses his message to communities rather than individuals. He reminds us that Christian life is communal. It is not about individuals striving for perfection. The idea of a private, personal religion would be totally foreign to him.

John is familiar with all the communities, suggesting he was an itinerant prophet who visited the churches he now addresses.[116]

Reflection:

1. What has been your experience with this book?

2. Why are the historical context and literary genre important for today's application?

LETTER TO THE SEVEN CHURCHES
(Rev. 1:1-3:22)

John received his inaugural vision while on the island of Patmos. He was told to write down his prophecy and send it to the churches of Ephesus, Smyrna, Pergamum, Thyatira, Sardis, Philadelphia and Laodicea. His message came directly from God.

In this first vision, John saw Jesus standing amidst the seven lamp stands (the seven churches). In other words, Jesus lived in the midst of His people. He was dressed in a long white robe (high priest) with a gold sash around his waist (royalty). His hair was white as wool or snow (ageless) and his eyes were burning flames (all knowing). His feet were like bronze (stable) and his voice like the sound of rushing waters (divine authority). In his right hand he held seven stars (angels of the seven churches, as well as universal dominion), and out of his mouth came a two-edged sword (God's word) and his face was shining like the sun (divine majesty). Overcome by such an experience, John fell to the ground much like Peter, James and John at the time of the Transfiguration.

John's apparition was a message of hope. Rome and all of its power could not compare to the authority and dignity of such a Redeemer, who even held the keys to the nether world. God's People had nothing to fear, not even death.

John then addressed each community, giving them Christ's assessment. The first letter went to Ephesus, the leading church in Asia Minor. The Ephesians were praised for not tolerating false apostles and the Nicolaitans, a group that probably advocated some sort of compromise with the prevailing culture. However, he chastised them because their initial charity seemed to have diminished.

John praised the Christians who lived in the wealthy city of Smyrna. Despite their poverty they were not seduced by riches, and maintained their integrity even though they were constantly harassed by a Jewish community who despised them.

Surrounding the city of Pergamum were numerous temples to the various Roman gods. The Christians were praised for remaining faithful, but chastised for allowing some members into their community, who advocated compromise in worship and eating food sacrificed to idols.

The city of Thyatira was a military outpost for Pergamum. The Christians were praised for their love and service, but chastised for allowing a prophetess in their midst, who encouraged them to accommodate the Roman deities.

The city of Sardis, though twice defeated in battles, was well protected. John used this history to challenge the false security of the community he described as being asleep. He attempted to shock them into awareness so that when Christ returned they would be prepared.

The Philadelphians were poor, but remained faithful. Christ would keep them safe through the bitter trials to come. They would occupy the places of honor in the heavenly Jerusalem.

The Laodiceans were utterly devoid of merit. They were seduced by the material wealth of the city. In their own eyes they lacked nothing, but in the eyes of their Lord they were lukewarm and would be vomited out of his mouth.

The letters to the seven churches were addressed symbolically to the entire Church. Every Christian assembly could see itself in these communities. It may be a poor struggling church, one whose faith and love was strong like those of Smyrna and Philadelphia; it may be wealthy and complacent like Laodicea and Sardis in real danger of losing the faith completely; or it may be a mixture of the good and bad, a church in constant need of conversion and further purification. In any case, John's words provide a valuable communal examination of conscience.

Reflection:

1. John claimed a direct revelation from God, but so did David Koresh of the Branch Davidians in Waco, Texas. How do you discern the validity of private revelation?

2. How would you assess the religious communities with whom you are familiar?

WHO IS LORD OF THE WORLD?
(Rev. 4:1-5:14)

In order to appreciate this section of John's book, imagine the attitude of the first Christians toward the empire that controlled their lives. The entire known world was under the rule of a single man, possessing financial, political, religious and military might beyond imagination, and living in grandeur at the heart of the most magnificent city. Since Caesar was universally considered to be unmatched in strength and majesty, it was not surprising he came to be venerated as a god.

Reading these chapters, it is important to keep in mind that our understanding of Jesus as divine was a gradual development. The first Christians were Jews and strict monotheists. They accepted

Jesus as the promised messiah, but did not think of him as God. Once Paul started preaching the Gospel to the Gentiles, the Church's understanding of Jesus as divine began to develop. We see this clearly in the Gospel of John and in the Book of Revelation. The Divinity of Christ was not officially defined until the council of Nicea (325 CE).

In this second vision, John is no longer on the island of Patmos, but is transported to the door of heaven. As he looks inside, his experience is beyond normal discourse. He uses the power of poetic imagery in an attempt to console and strengthen his readers. "You think Caesar is powerful? Behold the majesty of our God!"

John uses a collage of magnificent jewels to describe the indescribable one sitting on the throne. A psychedelic display of rainbow colors, brilliant lightning and peels of thunder demonstrated a power beyond imagination. Before the throne were seven spirits, the fullness of God's spirit surrounded by twenty-four elders (12 tribes and 12 apostles) dressed in white robes with golden crowns on their heads. Around the throne were four mysterious creatures (Ezek. 1:4-12) representing the fullness of creation: the majesty of the lion, the strength of the bull, the intelligence of man and the lofty flight of the eagle. These symbolic creatures also came to represent the four gospels.

The four beings worshiped the One on the throne by proclaiming his holiness and eternal presence. The elders, taking off their crowns as a sign of their subservience, participated by praising God as the One who brought all things into being.

The first four verses of chapter five imply that the heavenly court was faced with a serious problem. Because of Satan's rebellion, all of creation was in turmoil and alienated from the source of its being. The scroll with the seven seals (totally secure) was a heavenly document that disclosed the destiny of the world. The events recorded in the scroll revealed the defeat of Satan, the judgment of the earth and the salvation of the faithful. Unfortunately, no one could be found who had the moral integrity to break open the seals. John's tears represented the agony of his people longing for a savior.

The crisis was resolved when the Lamb that was slain, Jesus, stepped forward to receive the scroll. He had seven horns (power) and seven eyes (wisdom) indicating that God's knowledge of all things now applied to Jesus, sharing completely the dominion of the Creator.

When the Lamb stepped forward to receive the scroll, the four living creatures and the twenty-four elders again prostrated themselves in worship. As John's vision continued, thousands of angels joined in the adoration. The singing came to a marvelous crescendo when all the creatures of the universe joined the chorus and praised God as Creator and Jesus as Savior.

The vision of chapter five was the Apocalypse's version of what other books of the New Testament called Jesus' exaltation at the right hand of the Father. The death of Jesus was a cosmic turning point marking the beginning of Satan's demise.

Reflection:

1. What are the forces that leave us feeling helpless?
2. How can the scroll that seals our lives be unlocked?

SEVEN SEALS AND SEVEN TRUMPETS

John could have ended his entire work at the end of chapter five, but the revelation he received was like a precious jewel that needed to be viewed from all sides. His work is like a great symphonic theme that is repeated by each section of the orchestra and ending in a magnificent crescendo. The seven seals and seven trumpets recap the same story of judgment, punishment and triumph.

The first four seals unleashed the famous horsemen of the apocalypse (Zech. 1:8ff). The white horse, symbolizing victory, referenced the Parthians who were skilled with the bow and constantly harassed the empire's Eastern borders, winning a major victory in 60 BCE. John envisioned the Parthians as God's instrument of destruction. [117] He also alluded to them in the sixth trumpet and sixth bowl. The Red, Black and Green horses symbolized war and its effects: bloodshed, famine and death.

Returning to the heavenly realm, the fifth seal portrays the souls of the martyrs lying under the altar (symbol of their sacrifice). They were given the white robes of victory and reassured that their deaths were not in vain. Justice was about to prevail.

The sixth seal, depicting a cosmic collapse, was so frightening that people from all walks of life begged for the mountains to fall upon them. By singling out the rich and the mighty, John assures his audience that no one is exempted by privilege, and that wealth and power carry special responsibilities.[118]

Before the seventh seal was opened, John had two more visions expressing the belief that God's people would avoid judgment and share in the heavenly worship. First, he comforted those who remained faithful with the assurance of divine protection. Those sealed for redemption were one hundred forty-four thousand from the twelve tribes, except the tribe of Dan, believed to be the origin of the future antichrist. The tribe of Manasseh, originally a member of the Josephites, was added to make up the difference.[119] The number symbolizes the New Israel, comprising an immeasurable number of people of every nation, race, and language. Dispelling any doubts that this represented the literal number of those who would be saved, John shared a second vision in which he saw a great multitude that was too vast to count.

When the Lamb opened the seventh seal, the whole cycle began all over again. Each of the seven angels with a trumpet unleashed another series of disasters upon the anti-God forces.

It is clear from reading the Book of Revelation that John saw in the Exodus experience a paradigm for understanding how God was going to free His new people from the Romans. The first trumpet of hail and fire mixed with blood was reminiscent of the seventh plague (Ex. 9:13-26.). The second trumpet recalled the first Egyptian plague when the Nile was turned into blood (Ex. 7:14-24). The plagues in the exodus story were directed against the land, crops, animals and the people of Egypt.

The partial destruction of the world envisioned in these four trumpets foreshadowed God's plan to do a total makeover of the earth. John believed there was a strong connection between human action and the state of the natural world. The Divine punishment was also intended to purify creation. [120]

The fifth trumpet (reminiscent of Joel 2) released powerful, horse-sized locusts attacking those not sealed, stinging like scorpions and causing so much pain that people would long for death. At the sound of the sixth trumpet, four angels chained at the Euphrates, land of the Parthians, are released to destroy one-third of humanity. Accompanying the angelic mission, the Parthian cavalry ride horses with lion heads breathing fire and sulfur that cause painful deaths. The vision evokes the recurring theme of the final battle.

John interrupts the trumpet sequence to describe his recommissioning (next meditation). The seventh trumpet returns focus to the heavenly realm, proclaiming the coming of God's reign. The twenty-four elders again prostrate themselves before the throne, worshipping God for vindicating those who remained faithful.

The seven seals and trumpets express John's belief that God desires to punish all evil forces and reward those who remain faithful in the midst of persecution and death.

John also depicts the anti-God forces as being so recalcitrant there is no possibility for repentance.

Reflection:

1. How does John's understanding of good and evil correspond to human experience?
2. How do you understand Divine justice?

THE DRAGON AND HARVEST

The second half of the Book of Revelation is introduced by a vision depicting a mighty angel giving John his next commission. Like the prophet Ezekiel, John was told to eat the scroll, which tasted sweet in his mouth but turned bitter in his stomach. God's victory over evil was assured, but would not be forthcoming. In this second half of the book, John gives a more detailed description of the end times.

Introducing Satan as the great red dragon prepared to do battle with God and His People, John used an old story common at the end of the first century. In the ancient myth, Python attempted to prevent Apollo, the son of Zeus, from coming to power. By order of Zeus, the north wind rescued the pregnant Leto by carrying her off to an island where Poseidon, god of the sea, protected her with waves. Not finding her, Python gave up his search.[121]

The birth of Apollo was associated with the mythical "golden age." Augustus, Nero and several Roman emperors claimed that they were the new Apollo, and that their reign revealed the idyllic age of Rome.

John Christianized this myth. When the great red dragon pursued the pregnant woman, she was given the wings of an eagle (Ex. 19:4) and flew into the wilderness where she gave birth to her child. John was telling his listeners that Christ, and not the emperor, was the one who ushered in the golden age of wisdom, peace and prosperity.[122]

In chapter 13, John reinterpreted Daniel 7 to introduce the beast. In his version, there was only one beast rising from the sea with characteristics of the four creatures described by Daniel. Like the dragon in chapter 12, the beast represented the forces of destruction, chaos and sterility living in the sea. On another level, John's readers would have recognized the beast as Rome and the emperor Nero. A pagan legend had Nero returning from the dead as the Antichrist to reclaim his power with the help of the Parthians. Contrary to Roman propaganda, portraying order and peace for the world, John's version shows that any alliance with Satan leads to pandemonium.

John then had a vision of a second beast rising from the earth that was given the authority of the first beast. This second creature represented the Roman governors, or the local political authorities in Asia Minor, who promoted emperor worship.

Using the numbers 666, John attempted to identify the beast as Nero, the first emperor to persecute Christians. In John's time, the letters of the alphabet were used as numbers as well as letters. The Hebrew letters of "Caesar Nero" add up to 666. The letters of his Latin name add up to 616, used in some manuscripts.[123] On another level, 666 symbolized total evil. The number seven was considered the perfect number. Six symbolized imperfection, and when repeated three times it referred to complete imperfection or wickedness.

The next vision in this series depicts the Lamb on Mt. Zion worshipped by 144,000 not defiled by women. John sees the battle with Rome as a holy war calling for sexual abstinence. Since the world was passing away, celibacy and the willingness to die for the faith were appropriate Christian responses.

John's view of the end times becomes more gruesome with each new apparition. In the final vision in this cycle, he depicts a harvest with a sickle-wielding angel and the wine press of God's wrath. These duel metaphors of harvest and vintage result in a sea of blood, the depth of a horse's bridle for 200 miles.

Reflection:

1. Who are our modern day beasts?

2. How much would you be willing to endure to protect the integrity of your beliefs?

SEVEN BOWLS AND FINAL BATTLES

The next series of visions become more graphic as John gives reign to his revenge fantasies. Repeating the theme of persecution, punishment and vindication, he encourages his readers to remain faithful because the end is near. The figure of the Lamb once slain is now replaced by the triumphal image of the Lord of Lords, dressed in blood-soaked battle robes, riding a white stallion and leading his army.

The seven bowls of wrath (Jer. 25:15-26), like the trumpets, recall God's intervention at the time of the Exodus. The first four bowls, reflecting various plagues, are poured out on the earth, sea, rivers and sun—the entire universe. The fifth bowl is poured out on Rome, the "throne of the beast". The sixth bowl, drying the Euphrates, again anticipates the Parthian invasion. The seventh bowl announces the final destruction of "Babylon". Following the seven scrolls and seven trumpets that destroy one-fourth and one-third of humanity respectively, the seven bowls destroy everything.

"Babylon" was Satan's primary instrument to promote evil in the world. In Chapter 17:9, John revealed to his readers that this great harlot was Rome, a city built on seven hills. Despite its universal control, John sees God destroying this powerful metropolis in one hour. Ignoring the fragile and transient character of humanity, Rome's fatal flaw was the illusory belief that her prosperity and power would endure forever. Following Rome's destruction, John describes the overwhelming grief experienced by kings, merchants and seafarers who became rich from their commercial and political intercourse with the great whore.[124]

The cyclical character of the Apocalypse is apparent in the ongoing rebellion of Satan. It was first described as the dragon's attack on the woman and revolt against God. After the devil was driven out of heaven by Michael, he empowered the beast to continue the war against the followers of Jesus on earth. In chapter 16, the devils assembled the kings of the earth to do battle at Megiddo, the scene of many decisive battles in antiquity.

Another vision depicts Christ bringing judgment upon the nations, capturing the beast and false prophet, and hurling them into the fiery lake. The next revelation envisions the imprisonment of Satan for 1,000 years while Christ, accompanied by those martyred for their faith, establishes his kingdom on earth. After the millennium, the Great Dragon is set free and immediately gathers an army for a final battle. God finally destroys him once and for all.

John's message is clear. The power of evil is irrepressible.[125] Even though Jesus has won the victory over the forces of chaos by his death and resurrection, the Prince of Darkness still rules this world. The senseless killing and violence in Iraq, Afghanistan, Darfur, Somalia, the Middle East and our own city streets says that we have not learned the lesson of the cross. People use religion in order to justify their distorted beliefs. The poor of the world continue to suffer needlessly because of greed. The peoples of this earth remain divided because of religious, ethnic, racial, sexual and political agendas.

As followers of Jesus, we must claim His victory and live in such a manner that reveals the fundamental belief that we are all children of

God despite the suffering that we will experience. This is how we participate in Christ's redemptive work.

Reflection:

1. How does Divine violence portrayed by John differ from his depiction of demonic violence?

2. What would you consider the greatest evil we confront on a daily basis?

THE NEW JERUSALEM

The Bible begins in the Garden of Eden and ends in the New Jerusalem. Adam and Eve were driven from the Garden because of their disobedience. The New Jerusalem awaits those who remained faithful to their calling as children of God.

In the Book of Revelation, John contrasts the New Jerusalem, the virgin bride, with Babylon, the Roman whore. The picture he paints staggers the imagination as he describes a total makeover. The former earth and heaven have passed away and the sea, symbolizing evil and chaos, no longer exists.

Constructed of pure gold, the heavenly city is formed in the shape of a perfect cube, 1,500 miles in width, length and height. Precious stones line the foundation of the walls. Because the whole metropolis is filled with the Divine presence, it eliminates the need for a temple. The sun and moon, God and the Lamb, are the unfailing sources of light and life.

Beneath God's magnificent throne flows the River of Life, watering the entire area. The plants produce fruit each month of the year, and the leaves serve as medicine. The gates are always open, but nothing profane can enter.

For those suffering persecution and facing death, John's vision was a great source of inspiration and consolation. Alluding to a similar vision, Paul tells his readers: "The sufferings of the present cannot compare to the glory that awaits those who are faithful (Rm. 8:18)."

Concluding these reflections on the Book of Revelation, here are some final observations.

1. Predicting the end of the world as we know it is beyond our human capacity. Paul was wrong (1Cor. 15:52), and John of Patmos was obviously wrong (Rev. 1:3). Throughout history numerous lives have been negatively impacted with false prognostications. We should heed the words of Jesus: "But of the day or hour, no one knows… but only the Father" (Mk. 13:32). Furthermore, we ought to live our lives in such a manner that the end of time becomes irrelevant.

2. John was writing to communities that felt powerless standing up to a superpower. His message was one of hope and encouragement. History has shown that those in power have frequently used this Book to justify "holy" wars. Once Christianity became the official religion of Rome, the cross turned into a sword. The image of the good shepherd carrying the sheep on his shoulders became the mighty warrior riding into battle. "My eyes have seen the glory of the coming of the Lord. He is trampling out the vintage with his terrible swift sword…" (Rev. 19:11-16).

3. In John's time, Gentile converts to Christianity could forgo the painful ordeal of adult circumcision and were not bound by the dietary Jewish laws or the strict observance of the Sabbath, but they were obliged to abstain from meat sacrificed to the pagan gods and forbidden to worship idols. These minimum rules meant that a Christian had to shun Roman coins stamped with the face of the emperor (the mark of the beast on one's hand). They could not participate in trade guilds, which opened their meetings with a prayer to one of the gods, and they could not share table fellowship with their pagan friends and relatives who ate the sacrificial meats. John firmly believed that anyone who compromised on any of these issues was a traitor to the faith.

4. Perhaps the most controversial passage in the Book is the meaning of the 1,000-year reign before Satan was released from captivity. There are those who believe that Jesus will literally return to earth to establish a millennial (1,000 year) kingdom. Others believe that He will return after the kingdom is established through the efforts of faithful Christians. Premillennialists tend to focus on Christ's coming. Postmillennialists focus on good works in the here and now.[126] Regardless of one's personal position, it is clear that John believed in a future resurrection for most Christians. Only those who died for their faith shared immediately in God's glory. The rest of the faithful will only rise when Christ returns. Sinners will experience a second death. It is important to realize that his theology of the end time contrasts with the imminent resurrection expressed in the Gospels of Luke and John.

5. The Book of Revelation should be read in the context of the other writings of the New Testament. John's attitude toward Rome conflicts sharply with the Gospels and the letters of Paul, which were much more accommodating. John's image of a vengeful God clashes with Jesus' message of non-violence, compassion and forgiveness.

6. Despite a history of controversy, Revelation was eventually accepted as inspired scripture because some early church fathers believed the apostle, John, son of Zebedee, was the author.

Though Rome was not destroyed as John predicted, his message of hope and encouragement is his lasting legacy. He also challenges us to examine our beliefs. How do we live the gospel values in a secular society without compromising the integrity of our faith?

Reflection:

1. Was John's vengeful attitude toward Rome and the description of its demise a legitimate revelation from God or a projection of his feelings of being powerless?

2. Do you see Jesus more as a good shepherd or warrior king? Why or why not, and what are the ramifications of those images?

EPILOGUE

I began this book with a series of reflections on Divine Images that have impacted our lives. Although there are a growing number of people who profess no religious affiliation, religious beliefs continue to influence us in a positive or negative manner on multiple levels.

Our major religious traditions have served millions of people extremely well throughout much of recorded history. They contain time-tested wisdom and provide the framework for our ethical and legal systems. Religion offers structure, discipline and social participation in community. However, these same traditions have also imparted the framework for evil when their underlying theologies were distorted.

The attack on America on September 11, 2001, and the many other acts of terrorism committed by Isis, Boko Haram and various other groups, were executed by deeply devoted people who believed they were carrying out the will of God.

It may be difficult to understand how the killing of innocent people has anything to do with any form of spirituality, but the history of various religions is filled with such examples. The Crusades and the Inquisition left thousands dead all in the name of God. Hitler was the leader of a Christian country that exterminated six million Jews. Northern Ireland witnessed decades of hatred and killing between Catholics and Protestants. Shiites and Sunnis continue to kill one another in Iraq and Syria. The list could go on, but the point is that religion has been used throughout history to justify our inhumanity to one another.

Charles Kimball, in his book *When Religion Becomes Evil,* lists five warning signs of corruption in religion. The first sign is the belief that my religion possesses the Absolute Truth. Other traditions may contain partial truth, but we have the fullness of truth. The arrogance of such a position is expressed in phrases like, "Outside the church there is no salvation," or "You cannot be saved unless you accept Jesus as your personal Lord and Savior." When we divide people into the saved and unsaved, the pure and impure, the righteous and the sinners, we create the conditions for violence in the name of God.

The second warning sign is the requirement for blind obedience. As we struggle with the mystery of existence and the challenges of living in an uncertain world, authentic religion engages the total person: emotionally, intellectually, physically and spiritually. When religion seeks to limit intellectual freedom and personal integrity in the name of obedience to the authority of institutional leadership, it becomes stagnate and oppresses the workings of the Holy Spirit. When religion demands obedience to a charismatic leader or becomes enslaved to a particular idea, it can easily develop the framework for hatred and destruction.

The third warning sign is the establishment of the "Ideal Time". Throughout history there have been those who have predicted the end of time. Such a belief becomes destructive when those who long for a new age attempt to bring about the rapture through mass suicide or Armageddon (final battle) by acts of violence that encourage war between Israel and the Muslim world. Believing that we are living in the end times also justifies our rape of the environment and neglect of the poor.

The fourth warning sign is that the end justifies the means. The torture of heretics, witches or non-Christians to force conversions or confessions defies basic Christian principles. The killing of innocent people by suicide bombers, drone strikes or shock and awe bombing is justified as necessary collateral damage in fighting a war against "crusaders," "terrorists" or evil countries. Those Christians who have destroyed clinics or murdered doctors who have performed abortions believed they were defending the defenseless.

The final warning sign is the Declaration of a Holy War against Jews, Protestants, Catholics, Muslims, Americans, Blacks, Women and

Gays. As long as we continue to view those who are different than ourselves as somehow less than human, we use our religious traditions to justify violence against them.

No person's identity is exhausted by his or her gender, race, ethnic origin, religion, national loyalty or sexual preference. We are all children of the same God and share a common humanity. We have more in common than we do in conflict. When we idolize our differences we distort this fundamental reality, and religion then becomes a tool for evil.

The term "Christian" has been co-opted by those with a very narrow understanding of the Biblical tradition. Understanding the Bible as God's direct revelation removed from human influence destroys the richness of spirituality that emerged from a communal context spanning twelve hundred years. Their literalists' views obscure the many literary expressions that are conveyed throughout these sacred books, and deny the development of human consciousness as it struggles with the mystery of God conveyed in the experiences of daily life. Such a view interprets the world negatively, fearing the influence of perceived attacks on core beliefs. The denial of scientific and historical evidence supporting evolution, climate change and Biblical formation, coupled with the cultural wars involving same-sex marriage, abortion and contraception, have created a siege mentality undermining mutual dialogue with the larger world.

Reacting to this mindset, many people have chosen to abandon institutional religion in order to continue their spiritual journey along a different path. Regardless of our faith or atheism, we are all searching for meaning, because there is a hunger for connection at the very core of our being.

My goal throughout this manuscript was to convey some of the richness of Biblical spirituality and how it can impact our lives.

Appendix I

THE MIGHTY ACT OF GOD (Yawist and Priestly **Traditions)***

13:20 Setting out from Succoth, they camped at Etham near the edge of the desert. 21 The lord preceded them, in the daytime by means of a column of cloud to show them the way, and at night by means of a column of fire to give them light. Thus they could travel both day and night. 22 Neither the column of cloud by day not the column of fire by night ever left its place in front of the people.

14:1 Then the Lord said to Moses, 2 "Tell the Israelites to turn about and camp before Pi-hahiroth, between Migdol and the sea. You shall camp in front of Baal-zephon, just opposite, by the sea. 3 Pharaoh will then say, "The Israelites are wandering about aimlessly in the land. The desert has closed in on them. 4 Thus will I make Pharaoh so obstinate that he will pursue them. Then I will receive glory through Pharaoh and all his army, and the Egyptians will know that I am the Lord." This the Israelites did.

5 When it was reported to the King of Egypt that the people had fled, Pharaoh and his servants changed their minds about them. "What have we done!?" they exclaimed. "Why, we have released Israel from our service!" 6 So Pharaoh made his chariots ready and mustered his soldiers; 7 six-hundred first-class chariots and all the other chariot of Egypt with warriors on them all.

8 So obstinate had the Lord made Pharaoh that he pursued the Israelites even while they were marching away in triumph. 9 The Egyptians then pursued them; Pharaoh's whole army, his horse, chariots and charioteers, caught up with them as they lay encamped by the sea, at Pi-hahiroth in front of Baal-zephon.

10 Pharaoh was already near when the Israelites looked up and saw that the Egyptians were on the march in pursuit of them. In great fright they cried out to the Lord.

10b and the people of Israel cried out to the Lord.

11 And they complained to Moses, "Were there no burial places in Egypt that you had to bring us out here to die in the desert? Why did you do this to us? Why did you bring us out of Egypt? Did we not tell you this in Egypt when we said, "Leave us alone. Let us serve the Egyptians"? Far better for us to serve the Egyptians than to die in the desert." **13 But Moses answered the people, "Fear not! Stand your ground, and you will see the victory the Lord will win for you today. These Egyptians whom you see today you will never see again. 14 The Lord himself will fight for you; you have only to keep still."**

15 then the Lord said to Moses, why are you crying out to me: Tell the Israelites to go forward. 16 And you, lift up your staff and, with hand outstretched over the sea, split the sea in two, that the Israelites may pass through it on dry land. 17 But I will make the Egyptians so obstinate that they will go in after them. Then I will receive glory through Pharaoh and all his army, his chariots and charioteers. 18 the Egyptians shall know that I am the Lord, when I receive glory through Pharaoh and his chariots and charioteers."

19 the angel of God, who had been leading Israel's camp, now moved and went around behind them. **The column of cloud also, leaving the front, took up its place behind them, 20 so that it came between the camp of the Egyptians and that of Israel. But the cloud now became dark, and thus the night passed without the rival camps coming any closer together all night long.**

21a then Moses stretched out his hand over the sea;

21b and the Lord swept the sea with a strong east wind throughout the night and so turned it into dry land,

When the water was thus divided, the Israelites marched into the midst of the sea on dry land with the water like a wall to their right and to their left. 23 the Egyptians followed in pursuit; all Pharaoh's horses and chariots and charioteers went after them right into the midst of the sea.

24 In the night watch just before dawn the Lord cast through the column of the fiery cloud upon the Egyptian force a glance that threw it into a panic; 25 and he so clogged their chariot wheels that they could hardly drive. With that the Egyptians sounded the retreat before Israel, because the Lord was fighting for them against the Egyptians.

26 then the Lord told Moses, "Stretch out your hand over the sea, that the water may flow back upon the Egyptians, upon their chariots and their charioteers." 27 so Moses stretched out his hand over the sea

27b, and at dawn the sea flowed back to its normal depth. The Egyptians were fleeing head on toward the sea, when the Lord hurled them into its midst.

28a As the water flowed back it covered the chariots and the charioteers of Pharaoh's whole army which had followed the Israelites into the sea.

28b Not a single one of them escaped.

29 but the Israelites had marched on dry land through the midst of the sea, with the water like a wall to their right and to their left.

30 thus the Lord saved Israel on that day from the power of the Egyptians. When Israel saw the Egyptians lying dead on the seashore, 31 and beheld the great power that the Lord had shown against the Egyptians, they feared the Lord and believed in him and in his servant Moses.[127]

Appendix II
Gilgamesh Epic

The gods decided to flood the earth. But Ea, god of fresh water, whispered to the reed walls of my house the plans of Enlil, Leader of the Divine Assembly.

"Take specimens of every living thing on board. Make the ark as wide as it is long (Gn. 6:11-21), with a roof like the dome of the heavens".

First I built the hulls of the ark 175 feet high and the decks 175 feet wide… Then I caulked the ark with bitumen and asphalt thinned with oil. (Gn. 6: 14-16).

For six days and nights the winds blew. On the seventh day the raging storm subsided and the sea grew quiet. I felt the stillness and then realized everyone else had drowned in the flood. I opened the hatch, and sunlight fell on my face. I bowed my face to the deck and wept with tears running down my cheeks (Gn. 7:24-8:3)

The ark ran aground on Mt. Nisir. It remained grounded for six days, and then on the seventh day I released a dove. It flew back and forth, but came back without finding a place to rest. Then I released a swallow, but it also returned without finding a place to rest. Finally, I released a raven. Because the flood waters had begun to subside, the raven fed, circled, cawed and flew away. Immediately I released the rest of the creatures from the ark and they scattered to the four winds (Gn. 8:5-17).[128]

Appendix III

MARK

It happened in those days that Jesus came from Nazareth of Galilee and was baptized in the Jordan by John.

MATTHEW

Then Jesus came from Galilee to John at the Jordan to be baptized by him. John tried to prevent him by saying: "I need to be baptized by you and yet you are coming to me?" Jesus said to him in reply, "Allow it now, for thus it is fitting for us to fulfill all righteousness." Then he allowed him.

LUKE

…because all of the evil deed Herod had committed, added still another to these by (also) putting John in prison.

After all the people had been baptized and Jesus also had been baptized and was praying, heaven was opened and the Holy Spirit descended upon him in bodily form like a dove.

JOHN

The next day he saw Jesus coming toward him and said, "Behold the Lamb of God who takes away the sin of the world. He is the one of whom I said, "A man is coming after me who ranks ahead of me because he existed before me… Now I have seen and certify that he is the Son of God."

Bibliography

Anderson, B. W. (1975). *Understanding the Old Testament: Third Edition.* Englewood Cliffs, NJ: Prentice-Hall.

Armstrong, K. (1993). *A History of God: The 4000 Year Quest of Judaism, Christianity and Islam.* New York, NY: Ballantine Books.

Bailey, K. E. (1983). *Poet & Peasant and Through Peasant Eyes.* Grand Rapids, MI: William B. Eerdmans.

Bailey, K.E.(2008). *Jesus Through Middle Eastern Eyes.* Downers Grove, IL: InterVarsity Press.

Bailie, G. (1995). *Violence Unveiled.* New York, NY: The Crossroad Publishing Company.

Bergant, D. C.S.A.(1984) *What are they saying about wisdom literature* Ramsey, NJ: Paulist Press

Bergant, D. C.S.A. (1982) *Job, Ecclesiastes.*Wilmington, DE: Michael Glazier, Inc.

Boadt, L. (1984). *Reading the Old Testament: An Introduction.* New York, NY: Paulist Press.

Boadt, L. (1982). *Jeremiah 1-25.*Wilmington, DE: Michael Glazier, Inc.

Borg, M.J. (2012). *Evolution of the Word.* New York, NY: Harper Collins.

Borg, M. J. (1997). *The God We Never Knew: Beyond Dogmatic Religion to a More Authentic Contemporary Faith.* New York, NY: Harper Collins.

Boucher, M. I. (1981). *The Parables.* Wilmington, DE: Michael Glazier, Inc.

Brown, R. (1987). *An Adult Christ at Christmas.* Collegeville, MN: The Liturgical Press.

Brown, R. (1988). *A Coming Christ in Advent.* Collegeville, MN: The Liturgical Press.

Brown, R. E. (1984). *The Churches The Apostles Left Behind.* New York/Ramsey, NJ: Paulist Press.

Brown, R. E. (1988). *The Gospel and Epistles of John.* Collegeville, MN: The Liturgical Press.

Brueggemann, W. (1982) *The Prophetic Imagination* Philadelphia, PA: Fortress Press.

Brueggemann, W. (1982). *1 Kings.* Atlanta, GA: John Knox Press.

Brueggemann, W. (1982). *2 Kings.* Atlanta, GA: John Knox Press.

Brueggemann, W. (1982). *Genesis: Interpretation.* Atlanta, GA: John Knox Press.

Brueggemann, W. (1985). *David's Truth: In Israel's Imagination and Memory.* Philidelphia, PA: Fortress Press.

Brueggemann, W. (1987). *Hopeful Imagination: Prophetic Voices in Exile.* Philadelphia, PA: Fortress Press.

Brueggemann, W. (1988). *Jeremiah 1-25: To Pluck Up, To Tear Down.* Grand Rapids, MI: William B. Eerdmans Publishing.

Brueggemann, W. *(1989). Truth Speaks to Power: The Countercultural Nature of Scripture.* Louisville, KY: John Knox Press.

Brueggemann, W. (2003). *An Introduction to the Old Testament: The Canon and Christian Imagination.* Louisville, KY: Westminster John Knox Press.

Brueggemann, W. (2014). *Sabbath as Resistance: Saying No to the Culture of Now.* Louisville, KY: Westminster John Knox Press.

Burns, R. J. (1983). *Exodus, Leviticus, Numbers.* Wilmington, DE: Michael Glazier, Inc.

Clifford, R. (1982). *Deuteronomy.* Wilmington, DE: Michael Glazier, Inc..

Cody, A. O.S.B. (1984). *Ezekiel,* Wilmington, DE: Michael Glazier, Inc.

Collins, A. Y. (1979). *The Apocalypse.* Wilmington, DE: Michael Glazier, Inc.

Conroy,C.M.(1983). *1-2 Samuel, 1-2 Kings.*Wilmington, DE: Michael Glazier, Inc.

Crossan, J. D. (1989). *The Birth of Christianity:Discovering What Happened in the Years Immediately after the Execution of Jesus.* New York, NY: Harper Collins.

Crossan, J. D. (1992). *The Historical Jesus: The Life of a Mediterranean Jewish Peasant.* New York, NY: Harper Collins.

Crossan, J. D. (1994). *Jesus: A Revolutionary Biography.* New York, NY: Harper Collins.

Crossan, J. D. (2007). *God & Empire:Jesus Against Rome, Then and Now.* New York, NY: Harper Collins.

Crossan,J.D. and Borg, M.. (2009). *The First Paul: Reclaiming the Radical Visionary Behind the Church's Conservative Icon.* New York, NY: Harper Collins.

Crossan,J.D. and Borg,M . (1989). *The First Christmas.* New York, NY: Harper Collins.

Crossan,J.D. and Borg, M (2006). *The Last Week: What the Gospels Really Teach About Jesus's Final Days in Jerusalem.* New York, NY: Harper Collins.

Crossan,J.D. and Reed, L.R.(2004) *In Search of Paul.* San Francisco, CA: Harper Collins..

Ehrman, B.D. (2003) *Lost Christianities.* New York, NY: Oxford University Press

Ehrman, B.D.(2000).*The New Testament Course Guidebook.* Chantilly, VA: The Teaching Co.

Ellis, P. (1968). *The Yahwist: The Bible's First Theologian.* Collegeville, MN: The Liturgical Press.

Gilles, A. (1983). *The People of the Book.* Cincinnati, OH: St. Anthony Messenger Press.

Gillis, A. E. (1984). *Fundamentalsm: What Every Catholic Needs to Know.* Cincinnati, OH: St. Anthony Press.

Gorman, M. (2004). *Apostle of the Crucified Lord.* Grand Rapids, MI: William B. Eerdmans.

Harrington, D.S. (1981). *Interpreting the Old Testament.* Wilmington, DE: Michael Glazier, Inc.

Hays, E. (1986). *St. George and the Dragon.* Easton, KS: Forest of Peace Books, Inc.

Hoppe, L., O.F.M. (1982). *Joshua, Judges.* Wilmington, DE: Michael Glazier, Inc.

Jensen, J. (1984). *Isaiah 1-39.* Wilmington, DE : Michael Glazier, Inc.

Johnson, E. A. (2007). *Quest For The Living God: Mapping Frontiers in the Theology of God.* New York, NY: Continuum International.

Kimball, C. (2002). *When Religion Becomes Evil.* San Francisco, CA: Harper Collins.

Kirsch, J. (2006). *A History of the End of the World.* San Francisco, CA: Harper Collins.

Leary, J. F. (1979). *Hear, O Israel: A Guide to the Old Testament.* Walwick, NJ: Arena Lettres.

Lensky, G. (1966), *Power and Privilege: A Theory of Social Stratification*, New York, NY: McGraw-Hill.

Malone, M. (2001). *Women & Christianity.* New York, NY: Orbis Books.

Matthews, V. H.and Benjamin. D.C. (1991). *Old Testament Parallels: Laws and Stories from the Ancient Near East.* New York/Mahmah, NJ: Paulist Press.

Meier, R. E.and Brown, R., (1983). *Antioch & Rome: New Testament Cradles of Catholic Christianity.* New York/Ramsey, NJ: Paulist Press.

O'Connor, J.M., OP. (1982). *Becoming Human Together.* Wilmington, DE: Michael Glazier, Inc.

Pagels, E. (1979). *The Gnostic Gospels.* New York, NY: Random House.

Powell, M. A. (1998). *Jesus: How Modern Historians View the Man from Galilee* Louisville, KY: Westminster John Knox Press.

Sanders, J. A. (1972). *Torah & Canon.* Philadelphia, PA: Fortress Press:Louisville,KY: Westminster John Knox Press.

Schillebeeckx, E. (1979). *Jesus: An Experiment in Christology.* New York, NY: Crossroad.

Scullion,J. SJ. (1982). *Isaiah 40-66.*Wilmington, DE: Michael Glazier, Inc.

Stuhlmueller,C., C.P.(1983) *Psalms 1.* Wilmington, DE: Michael Glazier, Inc.

Stuhlmueller,C., C.P.(1985) *Psalms 2.* Wilmington, DE: Michael Glazier, Inc.

Vaux, R. \ (1958). *Ancient Israel: Social Institutions.* New York, NY: McGraw-Hill Book Co.

Winter, T. (2009). *Paradoxology: Spirituality in a Quantum Universe.* New York, NY: Orbis Books.

Endnotes

[1] Unless otherwise noted all Biblical quotations are from the *New American Bible* (Copyright 2006), DeVore and Sons, Inc., Wichita, Kansas 67201

[2] Translation by Leonard Bernstein *Mass*

[3] Pagels, Elaine, *The Gnostic Gospels* (New York: Vintage Books, 1979) p.60

[4] *De Virginibus Verlandis IX*

[5] Brueggemann, Walter, *Truth Speaks to Power* (Louisville, KY: Westminster John Knox Press, 1989) pp. 33-35.

[6] Crossan, John Dominic, *The Birth of Christianity: Discovering What Happened in the Years Immediately Following the Execution of Jesus* (San Francisco: Harper Collins,1998) p.189

[7] Ibid., 189

[8] Ibid.,190-191

[9] Ibid.,195

[10] Ibid.196

[11] Sanders, James, *Torah and Canon* (Philadelphia: Fortress Press, 1981) pp. 24-27.

[12] Brueggemann, Walter, *First and Second Samuel: Interpretation, A Bible-Commentary for Teaching and Preaching* (Louisville, KY: John Knox Press, 1990) p.63

[13] Ibid.,256-258

[14] Anderson, Bernhard, *Understanding the Old Testament: Third Edition* (Englewood Cliffs, NJ: Prentice Hall,1975) pp.184-186

[15] Ibid.,195-197

[16] Brueggemann, Walter, *An Introduction to the Old Testament* (Louisville, KY: Westminster John Knox Press,2003) p.146

[17] Brueggemann, Walter, *The Prophetic Imagination* (Philadelphia: Fortress Press, 1982) p.13

[18] Sanders, *Torah and Canon,* pp.78-89

[19] Brueggemann, Walter, *Truth Speaks to Power* (Louisville, KY: John Knox Press, 2013) p.101

[20] Ibid.,110

[21] Leonard Bernstein's *Mass*

[22] Leary, James, *Hear, O Israel: A Guide to the Old Testament* (Waldwick, NJ: Arena Lettres, 1979) p.69

[23] Ibid.,71

[24] Anderson, Bernhard W. *Understanding the Old Testament,* pp.287-288

[25] Ibid., p.330

[26] Ibid.,400

[27] Ibid.,416

[28] Boadt ,Lawrence, *Reading the Old Testament: An Introduction* (Mahwah,NJ: Paulist Press,1984) p.114

[29] Matthews,Victor H.and Benjamin, Don C., *Old Testament Parallels: Laws and Stories from the Ancient Near East*

(Mahwah,N.J.: Paulist Press,1991) pp.12,13)

[30] Brueggemann, Walter, *Genesis, Interpretation: A Bible Commentary for Teaching and Preaching* (Atlanta, GA.: John Knox Press, 1982) p.35

[31] Ibid.,44

[32] Ibid.,46

[33] Ibid., 48-49

[34] Ibid.,46

[35] Ibid., 60

[36] Ibid. pp.,76-82

[37] Ibid., 87

[38] Ibid., 102

[39] Leonard Bernstein's *Mass*

[40] Boadt, Lawrence, *Reading the Old Testament: An Introduction*, p.280

[41] St. Augustine *Confessions*

[42] Boadt, Lawrence, ,*Reading the Old Testament: An Introduction*, p.283

[43] Bergant, Diane, C.S.A., *What are They Saying About Wisdom Literature*, (Ramsey, N.J.: Paulist Press,1984) p.20

[44] Anderson, Bernhard, *Understanding the Old Testament*, p.542

[45] Crossan, John Dominic, *Jesus: A Revolutionary Biography*, (San Francisco: Harper Collins, 1989) p.68

[46] Brueggemann, Walter, *An Introduction to the Old Testament: The Canon and Christian Imagination* (Louisville, KY,2003) p.171

[47] Boadt, Lawrence, *Reading the Old Testament: An Introduction,* p.444

[48] Brueggemann, Walter, *Sabbath and Resistance: Saying No to the Culture of Now,*(Louisville, KY.: Westminster John Knox Press, 2014) pp.53-54

[49] Crossan, John Dominic, *The Historical Jesus: The Life of a Mediterranean Jewish Peasant,* (San Francisco: Harper Collins,1992) pp.237,238)

[50] Borg, Marcus, *Jesus: Uncovering the Life, Teachings, and Relevance of a Religious Revolutionary* (New York, NY: Harper Collins, 1989) p.134

[51] Ehrman, Bart D., *Lost Christianities* (New York, NY: Oxford University Publishing, 2003) pp.241,244

[52] Crossan,John Dominic, *God and Empire: Jesus Against Rome, Then and Now* (New York,,NY: Harper Collins (1989) pp.108-110

[53] Borg, Marcus, *Jesus: Uncovering, the Life, Teachings and Relevance of a Religious Revolutionary*, pp 186,187

[54] Borg, Marcus J. and Crossan, John Dominic, *The Last Week: What the Gospels Really Teach About Jesus's Final Days in Jerusalem,*(New York, NY: Harper Collins,2006) pp.2-3

[55] Ibid.,48

[56] Borg, Marcus, *Jesus: Uncovering the Life, Teachings, and Relevance of a Religious Revolutionary*, pp. 274,276

[57] Ibid.,92

[58] Bailey, Kenneth E., *Poet and Peasant: A Literary-Cultural Approach to the Parables of Luke* (Grand Rapids, MI: William B. Eerdmans Publishing (1976) pp. 161,181

[59] Hays, Edward, *St. George and the Dragon and the Holy Quest for the Grail* (Easton, KS: Forest of Peace Books,1986) pp105-107

[60] Bailie, Gil, *Violence Unveiled: Humanity at a Crossroad* (New York, NY: The Crossroad Publishing Company, 1999) pp.217,218

[61] I am indebted to Dr. Kenneth Bailey for providing the cultural context for this section.

[62] Bailey, Kenneth E. *Poet and Peasant*, pp.147,149

[63] Ibid.,155

[64] Ibid., 157

[65] Ibid., 157

[66] Ibid.,161

[67] Ibid.,168

[68] Ibid.,177

[69] Ibid.,181-182

[70] Ibid.185,186

[71] Ibid., 183

[72] Ibid.,194-195

[73] Bailey, Kenneth E. *Through Peasant Eyes* (Grand Rapids, MI: William B. Eerdmans Publishing, 1980) pp.44,45

[74] Ibid.,46

[75] Ibid.,48

[76] Ibid.,145,146

[77] Ibid.,148

[78] Ibid.,152

[79] Ibid.,153

[80] Bailey, Kenneth E. „Jesus Through Middle Eastern Eyes: Cultural Studies in the Gospels* (Downers Grove, IL: InterVarsity Press, 2008) p.384

[81] Ibid.,394

[82] Bailey, Kenneth E., *Through Peasant Eyes*, p.5

[83] Ibid.,8,9

[84] Ibid.,21

[85] Ibid.,94

[86] Ibid.,96

[87] Ibid.,97,98

[88] Ibid.,98,99

[89] Ibid.,108

[90] Brown, Raymond, E. and Meier John P.,*Antioch and Rome* (Ramsey, N.J.: Paulist Press,1983) pp.2,3,4,6

[91] Gorman, Michael J., *Apostle of the Crucified Lord* (Grand Rapids, MI: William B. Eerdmans Publishing Company, 2004) p.4

[92] Lenski, Gerhard E., *Power and Privilege: A Theory of Social Stratification* (New York,, NY: McGraw-Hill, 1966) pp.189-296

[93] Gorman, Michael J., *Apostle of the Crucified Lord* p.6

[94] Ibid.,7

[95] Borg, Marcus J. and Crossan, John Dominic, *The First Christmas: What the Gospels Really Teach About Jesus' Birth* (New NY: Harper Collins,2007) pp. 62-65

[96] Ehrman, Bart D. ,*The New Testament: Course Guidebook* (Chantilly, VA: The Teaching Company, 2000) p.12

[97] Ibid,.p.11

[98] Borg, Marcus and Crossan, John Dominic, *The First Paul: Reclaiming the Radical Visionary Behind the Church's Conservative Icon* (New York, NY: Harper Collins, 2009) p.14

[99] Ibid.,31-48

[100] Ibid.,51,52

[101] Ibid.,57

[102] Ibid.,53-56

[103] O'Connor, Jerome Murphy, OP, *Becoming Human Together: A Pastoral Anthropology of St. Paul* (Wilmington, DE: Michael Glazier Inc, 1984) p.115

[104] Ibid.,pp.116,117

[105] Ibid.,97

[106] Ibid.,84,85

[107] Gorman, Michael, *Apostle of the Crucified Lord*, pp.102-105

[108] O'Connor, Jerome Murphy, OP, *Becoming Human Together*, p.43

[109] Ibid., p.166

[110] Crossan, John Dominic and Reed, Jonathan L., *In Search of Paul: How Jesus's Apostle Opposed Rome's Empire with God's Kingdom* (San Francisco: Harper Collins, 2004) pp.38-40

[111] O'Connor, Jerome Murphy, OP, *Becoming Human Together*, p.174

[112] Ibid.,p.190

[113] Kirsch, Jonathan, *A History of the End of the World* (San Francisco: Harper Collins, 2006) p.64

[114] Ibid.,68

[115] Ibid.,70

[116] Ibid.,66

[117] Collins, Adela Yarbro, *The Apocalypse,* (Wilmington, DE: Michael Glazier, Inc., 1979.) pp.44-45

[118] Ibid.,p.49

[119] Ibid.,52,53

[120] Ibid.,59

[121] Ibid.,86

[122] Ibid.,86

[123] Kirsch, Jonathan, *A History of the End of the World,* p.83

[124] Collins, Adela Yarbro, *The Apocalypse*, pp.127-128

[125] Ibid.,141

[126] Kirsch Jonathan, *History of the End of the World*, p.189

* Yahwist in bold, Priestly in regular print

[127] Ellis, Peter, The Yahwist: *The Bible's First Theologian* (Collegeville, MN: The Liturgical Press, 1968) p.38

[128] Matthews, Victor H..and Benjamin, Don C., *Old Testament Parallels: Laws and Stories from the Ancient Near East*, (New York/Mahwah, NJ: Paulist Press, 1991) pp.35-36

CPSIA information can be obtained at www.ICGtesting.com
Printed in the USA
BVOW01s1430050816

457914BV00004B/18/P